SENT...

Copyright © 2023 by Märt Vähi

Published by Four Rivers Media

All rights reserved. No portion of this book may be reproduced, stored in a retrieval system, or transmitted in any form or by any means—electronic, mechanical, photocopy, recording, scanning, or other—except for brief quotations in critical reviews or articles, without prior written permission of the author.

Unless otherwise specified, Scripture quotations are taken from the (NASB®) New American Standard Bible®, Copyright © 1960, 1971, 1977, 1995, 2020 by The Lockman Foundation. Used by permission. All rights reserved. www.lockman.org | Scripture quotations marked AMP are taken from the Amplified® Bible (AMP), Copyright © 2015 by The Lockman Foundation. Used by permission. www.lockman.org | Scripture quotations marked AMPC are taken from the Amplified® Bible (AMPC), Classic Edition, Copyright © 1954, 1958, 1962, 1964, 1965, 1987 by The Lockman Foundation. All rights reserved. Used by permission. www.lockman.org | Scripture quotations marked ERV are taken from the East-to-Read Version of the Bible. Copyright © 2006 by Bible League International | Scripture quotations marked KJV are taken from the King James Version of the Bible. Public domain. | Scripture quotations marked MSG are taken from THE MESSAGE, copyright © 1993, 1994, 1995, 1996, 2000, 2001, 2002 by Eugene H. Peterson. Used by permission of NavPress. All rights reserved. Represented by Tyndale House Publishers, Inc. | Scripture quotations marked NIV are taken from the Holy Bible, New International Version®, NIV®. Copyright © 1973, 1978, 1984, 2011 by Biblica, Inc.™ Used by permission of Zondervan. All rights reserved worldwide. www.zondervan.com. The "NIV" and "New International Version" are trademarks registered in the United States Patent and Trademark Office by Biblica, Inc.™ | Scripture quotations marked NKJV are taken from the New King James Version®. Copyright © 1982 by Thomas Nelson. Used by permission. All rights reserved. | Scripture quotations marked NLT are taken from the Holy Bible, New Living Translation, copyright © 1996, 2004, 2015 by Tyndale House Foundation. Used by permission of Tyndale House Publishers, Inc., Carol Stream, Illinois 60188. All rights reserved. | Scripture quotations marked TPT are from The Passion Translation®. Copyright © 2017, 2018 by Passion & Fire Ministries, Inc. Used by permission. All rights reserved. ThePassionTranslation.com. | Scripture quotations marked WE come from the World English version of the Bible © 1969, 1971, 1996, 1998 by SOON Educational Publications, Willington, Derby, DE65 6BN, England. You may freely quote up to 500 verses of this New Testament without permission. Please credit them if possible as "Taken from THE JESUS BOOK–The Bible in Worldwide English. Copyright SOON Educational Publications, Derby DE65 6BN, UK. Used by permission."

For foreign and subsidiary rights, contact the author.

Cover design by Sara Young

ISBN: 978-1-960678-49-2   1 2 3 4 5 6 7 8 9 10

Printed in the United States of America

SENT...

THE AMAZING CONNECTION BETWEEN OUR DESTINY AND THE GUIDING PRINCIPLE OF THE LIFE OF CHRIST!

MÄRT VÄHI

Dedication

To all the wonderful men and women who, over my lifetime, have influenced, mentored, and inspired me to be who and where I am today.

CONTENTS

Acknowledgments ix

Introduction 11

CHAPTER 1. **Whose Way?** 15

CHAPTER 2. **You Were Born for and With a Purpose!** 21

CHAPTER 3. **Marching Orders** 47

CHAPTER 4. **To What or to Whom Are You Submitting Your Life?** .. 107

CHAPTER 5. **Whose Promotional Package Are You Unloading?** 141

CHAPTER 6. **Exclusive Rights** 183

Conclusion 223

ACKNOWLEDGMENTS

I had a friend Frank Costantino who asked me the question: "When you see a turtle on a fence post, what conclusion do you come to? The answer is quite obvious: "He did not get there by himself!"

I did not get to the top of this particular fence post—writing this book—by luck or fortune but by the conviction of what I write, inspired over the years, by those to whom I have dedicated this book and those who made it practically possible.

To my wife and best friend, Alta, for your encouragement throughout our lives and the countless hours of research and writing.

To Gorgina Wallace, school teacher and friend from years back, for working on my beginning manuscripts and for the early encouragement to write at all.

To my friend and coach, John F. Caplin, MA, Certified Executive Coach | Birkman Master Certified Professional; Tilt 365 Master Coach | Tilt 365 Team Consultant and Change Agent, for

SENT...

helping guide me through my many obligations, life goals, and daily activities, so I could make time to research and writing.

To Andrew, my son, together with the staff and people at Village of Hope in Canada and Estonia, for allowing me to take time from the busy daily activities of pioneering, building, and expanding this ministry for those in chemical addiction to research and write.

To Martijn van Tilborgh of Four Rivers Media and his wonderful professional staff who did so much to get this book practically off the ground and running.

To my Lord Jesus for the privilege of being SENT...

INTRODUCTION

As of the last several years, I have been totally absorbed by the words of Jesus: His sayings and teachings. I have, to say the least, been challenged, convicted, inspired, encouraged, enlightened, and excited, among a variety of positive reactions. On this point, I will not even begin to elaborate! But while on this, I came upon an unbelievable discovery and revelation so unexpectedly. This profound truth now forms the basis and purpose of this book. I want to zero in on one unbelievable, unique, and exciting truth I have discovered during my reading of what Jesus said and taught.

Here it is. Jesus says in John 20:21 (KJV): "As my Father hath sent me, even so send I you."

I have read it dozens of times before! In the ERV, this verse reads: "It was the Father who sent me, and I am now sending you in the same way." Actually, no matter what version you may be using, there is no doubt as to the clear meaning of the text, and the meaning never changes. Jesus is saying this in a comparative

SENT...

way. That raises its importance significantly as it relates to us in a very special and unique way.

I would draw your attention to the small words "as," "even so," and in the "same way." These are words of comparison. If Jesus had said, "I was sent by the Father" and "now I am sending you," these words of Jesus would not have had such an impact and implication as they now have when He uses the small but seemingly insignificant words *like as* and *even so*. These small words change everything, and as a result, the statement becomes extremely significant for you and me. What He is saying cannot really be taken any other way except exactly how it appears: "The Father has sent Me, and now, I am sending you in the same way." Comparatively speaking, we are sent in the "same way" He was sent, except now, by Jesus Himself.

If you and I want to know how we are sent by Jesus and what our response should be, then it would be extremely wise and important for us to pay close attention to how Jesus was sent by His Father and how He responded and related to this.

This is so important that you will see repeatedly occurring words italicized. This is my doing. I've done it intentionally, to show that emphasis has been added to the original verses.

By seeing where they occur and how they relate to verses with the same words, we can draw conclusions and compare notes to see how we are sent and how we should respond in turn. We have been sent and commissioned in an exact parallel manner to how Jesus was. It is a startling matter to consider! That is exactly what I started to do.

We have the Gospels for reference. I started in the book of John and have gone no further. A wealth of material still awaits, just

Introduction

throughout the rest of the Gospels alone. But, even in just the book of John, I have already come to some very startling conclusions of which I am still in the middle of discovering and am not even nearly finished.

Maybe, as we prayerfully read this book with all the world before us—thousands of opportunities and challenges, decisions waiting to be made on boards and committees, organizational planning and expansions to take place, and need for desperate solutions or achieved successes—we could ask ourselves some heart-searching questions.

In this book, I simply invite you into your own exploration on the subject to draw your own conclusions. I include examples from my own life as illustrations of practicality. In turn, my experiences may lend a hand that you can relate to, based on where you have been and are presently today. They may well answer the questions of where and how we all fit into the big picture of who really is in control of our lives, the adventures we have embarked upon, the prayers we pray, and the many thousand things we do. Who or what is the motivation behind all of this? What influences us? Perhaps, as so common to many, we are on a mission of our own, asking for God's help, support, and blessings? Who sent us? Whose idea was it to do what we are doing, how we are doing it, or where we are going to do it?

Hence the subject and title of this book: *SENT* . . . and the first chapter . . . *Whose Way?*

CHAPTER 1

WHOSE WAY?

On December 30, 1968, Frank Sinatra recorded his version of the song "My Way," which was released in early 1969 while I was in my first year of Bible school. Most will remember it, and many others will have heard it recalled in one way or another. The pop song reached No. 27 on the Billboard Hot 100 chart and No. 2 on the Easy Listening chart in the US. In the UK, the single achieved a still unmatched record, becoming the recording with the most weeks inside the Top 40 chart.[1]

It went on to be sung in various versions by top artists like Welsh singer Dorothy Squires, Elvis Presley, who began performing the song in concert during the mid-1970s, Sid Vicious, Chris Mann, British singer Samantha Jones, and the Pogues' Shane MacGowan. Additionally, Dutch singer and painter Herman Brood covered

---

1 "My Way," *Wikipedia*, updated May 15, 2023, https://en.wikipedia.org/wiki/My_Way.

SENT...

the song, and finally, "My Way" and Frank Sinatra are mentioned in the Bon Jovi song, "It's My Life."

So what started this, and why did it become popular? Perhaps the author of the lyrics, Paul Anka, who set it to the music based on the French song "Comme d'habitude" by Claude François, answers it best. In New York, Anka rewrote the original French song with English lyrics, specifically for Frank Sinatra. The words were actually unrelated to the original French song. He explains: "We were in the 'me generation' and Frank became the guy for me to use to say that."[2]

The lyrics are sung by a guy who has reached his end—his final curtain call. After all, what does a man have if he doesn't have himself? Nothing! He took great satisfaction in ending his life stating, "I did it my way!"[3]

> **COULD IT BE THAT THE "ME" GENERATION HAS, TO SOME DEGREE, ALWAYS EXISTED AND ALWAYS WILL?**

Perhaps that was one of the major factors of the full success of the song—the "Me" generation." Could it be that the "Me" generation has, to some degree, always existed and always will? It just seems to me that during the era of the latter 1960s, it just began to surface in the form of many things, including this song.

On the flip side of the coin, do you think Jesus would have concurred with this belief system? We can view one answer to this in John 12:24-25 (NLT):

---

[2] "Comme d'habitude," Wikipedia, updated April 10, 2023. https://en.wikipedia.org/wiki/Comme_d%27habitude.
[3] Frank Sinatra, vocalist: "My Way," by Paul Anka, released March 1969, Reprise Records.

Whose Way?

I tell you the truth, unless a kernel of wheat is planted in the soil and dies, it remains alone. But its death will produce many new kernels—a plentiful harvest of new lives. Those who love their life in this world will lose it. Those who care nothing for their life in this world will keep it for eternity.

Perhaps things were not so different in Jesus's time, where he may have well confronted a "Me" generation. In a number of places, Jesus shows us the way of submission, service, and surrender as a way of life to follow him. Mark 8:34 (NLT) says, "Then, calling the crowd to join his disciples, he said, 'If any of you wants to be my follower, you must give up your own way, take up your cross, and follow me.'"

Luke described it this way:

A large crowd was following Jesus. He turned around and said to them, "If you want to be my disciple, you must, by comparison, hate everyone else—your father and mother, wife and children, brothers and sisters—yes, even your own life. Otherwise, you cannot be my disciple. And if you do not carry your own cross and follow me, you cannot be my disciple. But don't begin until you count the cost. For who would begin construction of a building without first calculating the cost to see if there is enough money to finish it. . . . So you cannot become my disciple without giving up everything you own. Salt is good for seasoning. But if it loses its flavor, how do you make it salty again? Flavorless salt is good neither for the soil nor for the manure pile. It is thrown away. Anyone

SENT...

with ears to hear should listen and understand!" —Luke 14:26-28 and 33-35 (NLT)

To me, it does not sound much like Frank Sinatra's "My Way" or the "Me" generation principles are in effect to qualify as a disciple. Could it be that the generational philosophy of the late '60s has actually been with us from the very beginning of creation, extending even to this day? Perhaps from the beginning of time, there have been the Paul Ankas of the world who have written the lyrics of this belief system and the Frank Sinatras who have sung its songs in one fashion or another.

Yet at the same time, there is the call of God to follow the exact opposite principle, which echoes across the ages and reflects the very heart of God. We see it in Scripture; we see it in the life of Christ; we see it in the lives of those who have followed God in ages gone buy as well as followers of Christ in Scripture and history to this very day.

It challenges us to choose, not only once and with the expectation of final results, but to be exercised over and over again, because time and time again, we come to the crossroads of our thinking. It becomes a downright struggle to decide whether I am going to do it my way or God's way. Why is this a struggle for us as Christians?

I am positively sure every one of us, at face value, would agree we wish to do it God's way and not our own way, without struggle—right? Indeed, we would!

Whose Way?

> **I AM POSITIVELY SURE EVERY ONE OF US, AT FACE VALUE, WOULD AGREE WE WISH TO DO IT GOD'S WAY AND NOT OUR OWN WAY, WITHOUT STRUGGLE—RIGHT? INDEED, WE WOULD!**

So, what's the problem?

The problem is that it is not as easy as it seems. Many questions surface, which is what inspired this book. We do things so often out of various influences like certain customs, figures of speech, terminology, traditions, preferences, passed-down ideas, subconscious thinking, and even circumstances. Then to top it all off, we excuse ourselves with all kinds of world and even religious influences. The lists go on and on.

Who is really in control? Why do we do what we do? Who or what influences our decisions and our thinking in what we choose to do? Why do we make the decisions we do? Even Frank Sinatra himself had doubts:

> Although this work became Frank Sinatra's signature song, his daughter Tina Sinatra says the legendary singer came to hate the song. "He didn't like it. That song stuck and he couldn't get it off his shoe. He always thought that song was self-serving and self-indulgent."[4]

To stay about as relevant as I know how, I chose the unpretentious terminology to expand the thoughts behind this book and the title of this chapter to simply ask the question that only you can answer and God can judge: "Whose Way?"

---

4 "Entertainment | Sinatra 'loathed' My Way," *BBC News*, 30 Oct. 2000, news.bbc.co.uk/2/hi/entertainment/994742.stm.

CHAPTER 2

YOU WERE BORN FOR AND WITH A PURPOSE!

I stood with my bare feet in the cold waters of the Baltic Sea on the shallow, receding coastline of Hiiumaa Island, off the coast of the nation of Estonia, looking directly west into the setting sun as it formed a golden, simmering glow across the reflecting waters. I was totally absorbed, almost spellbound, and completely enthralled by the moment. An overwhelming sense of destiny gripped my heart. I was destined to be here—interested in much more than my own desires, motivation, plan, or design at this point and time of my life. I have woven a backdrop of my life into the fibers of this book, so you understand the convictions of what I believe the Bible and Christ say, not only as a lesson in

SENT...

theology, but a truth that I have experienced and walked through my entire life.

> **AS CHRIST'S LIFE WAS FILLED WITH A PURPOSE AND DESTINY, SO I BELIEVE YOURS AND MINE ARE.**

As Christ's life was filled with a purpose and destiny, so I believe yours and mine are. Through the sayings of Christ and His relationship with the Father and with us, He brings to the surface, visible for us to understand, formed in eternity along with time, the purpose He has designed for our lives. The nucleus of attention to this is in these words I've mentioned before: "Then said Jesus to them again, Peace be unto you: as my Father hath sent me, even so send I you" (John 20:21, KJV).

I am sure you have also stood in a moment of time, perhaps not with your feet in the ocean, but somewhere, at some place and time, you knew you were standing on the very face of your destiny—a plan and purpose far greater and extensive than you could have ever dreamed up in your mind. You could not have written it in your plan nor have had the power or tools to form your lot in life that is your destiny. Rather, you may have just been given a small glimpse into the purpose for which you were born. I'm not talking about any span of your imagination or creation, but something that God Himself created—a God thing!

DESTINED TO BE AND DO

As I stood there, my mind raced over time to a different scene. On September 27, 1944, on this very same coastline, nearing the end of World War II and fleeing the Red Army not many kilometers away, my parents and my tiny two-month-old sister boarded the three-masted old wooden cargo ship known as *Enge*. The old vessel, built in 1898, had just days earlier been taken out of being "mothballed" to make its escape journey to Sweden. The sailing vessel was a cargo schooner never designed for passengers, but on this day, it carried a precious cargo of 495 souls, all fleeing their beloved homeland from the Communists.

As if one thing after another, being fired upon by Soviet planes and confronted by a German U-Boat 676 were not enough, a raging storm well-known at this time of year in those regions had developed. This threw the *Enge* like a wounded soldier plunging recklessly forward with all odds for survival against him. It was not yet midnight, and everyone, especially the captain, knew deep down in their hearts that the aged vessel would soon break up to meet her doom and carry all those whom she held in her bosom to a watery grave. These people who had set out on a journey to freedom and safety were now to die here in a watery grave in the middle of the Baltic Sea? As Captain Onno swept his dimly fading battery torch over the human cargo in front of him, he could hear the crash of the waves against the wooden hull. What could he say? What was their hope?

Then in a voice that seemed to come from the depth of his own soul, he shouted with a conviction braced by the very pulses of his own heart:

> "This ship will not make it—it cannot stand this much longer! Our only help is God! If anyone on this ship knows how to pray—pray to God as He alone can save us!"

SENT...

His words boomed down the entire length of the human-filled hold and seemed to resound over and over, though he only spoke it once. With this, he turned and climbed the stairs, once again, to the deck above.

The words pierced my mother's heart to the core of her chilled soul. Though she had believed in God, she had never really prayed, except for some formal prayers in the Lutheran church she attended during confirmation and some other formal occasions. But to pray a prayer out of the desperation of her heart that could be the difference between life and death? She hardly knew where to begin. What was she to do, and how was she to pray? She was so deathly seasick—so feeble that she could not even look after her two-month-old child. Not able to stand on her feet, she dropped to her knees, clasped her hands together and prayed, the words flowing with emotion and desperation: "Lord, we need to get to Sweden! If we get to Sweden, I promise You I will go to church every Sunday!"

> **THOUGH MY MOTHER HAD BELIEVED IN GOD, SHE HAD NEVER REALLY PRAYED, EXCEPT FOR SOME FORMAL PRAYERS IN THE LUTHERAN CHURCH SHE ATTENDED DURING CONFIRMATION AND SOME OTHER FORMAL OCCASIONS.**

The storm raged throughout the night; it would be difficult to describe it. People sobbed, most of them seasick to no end. The vessel was barely holding its own, and every smash of the waves was as if it might be her last. Hope for all was at rock bottom. My mother felt as if she would pass out at any moment. My baby sister was not taking anything in and had developed diarrhea, growing very sick. Her situation was becoming life-threatening.

The night wore on, yet in the constant wind, waves, spray, and pounding, the *Enge* seemed to have gained a supernatural stability as if the hand of God had a grasp beneath its hull, keeping her from dipping under the surface of the angry sea, never to emerge again. The miraculous intervention of the divine power of God had shown up. It was without a doubt an answer to the desperate and frantic prayers of the souls onboard. And yet, was it something more? Did God have a plan and a purpose, a design that would allow me to look back on that day and realize the significance of the plan and destiny of God in my life—a life not yet even born?

Soon, daylight was beginning to break, and degree upon degree, the storm began to subside. It was calculated the ship had been completely blown off course, somewhere southeast of the islands at the entrance of the route to Stockholm. One shattered mast was down. The remaining battered and torn sails provided just enough strength to keep the ship barely moving. My mother now prayed not that they would make it to Sweden, because it now seemed a miracle was already happening, and perhaps her baby girl would live to see it happen.

Late in the afternoon, land was spotted nearby, and the neat and tidy red and bright yellow Swedish-style houses were clearly visible to those who had all clambered up to the deck of the sailing ship. My mother did not come on deck—she was deathly weak, and her baby lay motionless in her arms. A Swedish coast guard cutter helped guide the *Enge* starboard to the side of the dock.

SENT...

My mother was helped from the hold of the ship, her baby immediately taken by doctors to the waiting ambulance. She did not even see my dad until several days later. The doctors admitted that had it been just a matter of hours more, my sister would not have survived. She was close to complete dehydration.

The story goes on at great length. You can read it in my upcoming autobiography titled *Thank God for the Woodshed*. It weaves the story of my life from the basis of my birth in Sweden three years after this event.

I list some of these things in a very brief form which would hardly tell the tale and stories behind it all. Yet, I mention these things without hesitation and to reinforce the truth of God's direction and plan—it is full and exciting, and our lives will only become richer and fuller as we begin to understand His will, purpose, and calling. Every case is a win-win situation!

After immigration to Canada when I was four, I saw my mother healed in a miraculous way when I turned eight. This resulted in accepting Jesus into my heart that same year all because of the prayer my mother prayed that day in the rough cargo hold of the ship *Enge*. This was not only for her but for this boy who did not know anything about destiny, God's will, or His purpose. Yet I believe it was my mother's prayer that led her in the will of God in bringing her to Sweden. It was the ring that matched the chimes of heaven and lined up perfectly to the precast note of a sound born in God's destiny that was set before time in eternity itself and would weave an eternal divine cord of God's purpose and will throughout the numerous years and events in my own life.

At the age of thirteen, while praying in the old barn on our farm in the country, I felt the very call of God to preach the gospel.

As a kid growing up on the farm, I spent hours in the old barn praying and talking to God. We as children worked almost what seemed unreasonably hard with responsibilities tough to imagine for today's same-age kids. Yet, I studied the Bible and attended camp meetings and church services with every bit of fervency and passion. It is not just my story but the story of God meticulously entwined and woven into my life and my life into His. In simple terminology, I can see the "hand of God" in my life.

> **THERE IS A DESTINY THAT EXISTS FOR YOU INDEPENDENT OF CIRCUMSTANCES, SITUATIONS, OPINIONS, OR ANY SET OF CONDITIONS WHICH MAY SEEM TO BE RULING YOUR LIFE RIGHT NOW. JUST TAKE A CLOSER LOOK!**

I know in a similar way you can see it in yours. It may be different than mine, and no doubt it is. Nevertheless, it is the story of your destiny that brought you to where you are today. It may be a difficult series of events and tales. Without a doubt, there are sad and tragic incidences that gripped various episodes of your life. Perhaps you are in the middle of a few right now, and everything seems blurred and like they are running together, not making any sense. It may be just the opposite of this. Things are falling into place with great strides of success. Happy times and joyous moments highlight your days, events, and years. It could not be any better. Or, life may seem to be a drag and gray. Every day is a challenge, and nothing seems to change one way or another. Nothing bad is happening, yet nothing good is happening, either.

SENT...

You can be assured of one thing—God still has a plan for your life! There is a destiny that exists for you independent of circumstances, situations, opinions, or any set of conditions which may seem to be ruling your life right now. Just take a closer look!

DIVINE DESIGN

You see, it is not that we just happen to be, and then somehow along the way, we get God involved into our lives. No, God has a purpose and design for our lives. We submit to Him, turn to Him, and fall in line with what He has divinely designed for us, and He plans to work through us. It is all there and has always been there.

I entered Bible school, learned from great men of God, like E. P. Wickens and C. B. Dudley, preached regularly, and graduated from seminary. Then I traveled to Europe with a childhood best friend, Paul Prosser, and we spent time in Spain with great missionaries like Bill Drost and missionary statesmen like Wynn Stairs, Frank Kosik, and Ed Bradley who all impacted my life. In Holland, it was Peter Quist, Brother Andrew (author of *God's Smuggler*), and in Finland, Veikko Manninen, which led me to hair-raising tales of smuggling Bibles to the very land where my parents had escaped many years before and then into the rest of Eastern Europe. Finally returning from my adventures in Europe, I married a wonderful lady, Alta, who was every bit as passionate about missions and dedicated to serving Jesus as I was.

It is something we all face in every aspect of our lives. We are called to submit to His purpose, and thereby, we are releasing and unfastening the greatest potential of our lives. We will deal with this in the next chapter. But until we come to realize this, we will always be struggling to get God's best in our lives or somehow get His favor in order for Him to use us. So often, we get it all backwards. He already has a design and He has a will and plan all prepared for us, so we can step into the greatest possible potential for our lives. We come into this by submission. Yes, submission to His plan for our lives. It is neither achieved by trying to coax God or convince Him somehow that He should actually use us in some unique way nor by talking Him into approving some kind of a plan we have thought up and developed, no matter how good it may seem.

Submitting to His plan is something that is already set in place before time or circumstances even existed. His ways are already in motion, in full swing, because they were meticulously formulated and harmoniously arranged. His plan set the stage of life, like a legendary piece of music waiting to be played by the orchestra of your life. Simply accepting this is what I mean when I say, "You were born for and with a purpose!"

This does not mean all will be easy, but it means it is for the best—the best it could ever possibly be. I experienced this. I pastored for a season in Eastern Canada, in the harbor city of Saint John but soon was back in Europe. It was the persistent inner call, the direction of the Holy Spirit, creating an urgent conviction to do what my wife and I needed to do. Upon the direction of Christ in our lives, we would carry thousands of Bibles through the Iron Curtain. We would travel even into the interior of the Soviet Union as far south as Armenia and, of course, north to Estonia. We did this together and eventually had three small children who would travel thousands of miles with us, enduring all kinds of impossible situations and circumstances. God spoke to others and eventually, with several teams working together, we would see tens of thousands of Bibles cross the borders over a seven-year period.

SENT...

Finally, in 1977, we were arrested coming out of the Soviet Union in Moldovia. There were hours of interrogations, threats, and uncertainties. My wife stood strong, not giving an inch. We did not lie but at the same time, would not admit to any of their accusations, no matter the pressures. Finally, my wife and I, along with our children ages one, two, and four, were sentenced by a Soviet court to prison. Unable to keep a family in prison, we were instead expelled from the Soviet Union for life. All our team members had also been arrested just prior to this with the same fate.

In a moment like this, it seemed that all had somehow gone so terribly wrong. The temptation to wonder how we might have missed it was there. But in a time like this, you shouldn't let your thinking take over. Instead, you stick to what God has said and push through with raw faith and conviction that God is still in charge, and it will be okay. There are many moments when fear and thinking in the natural can come like an onslaught. It feels possible you will lose direction, yet this is never an option. It is times like these that we test what God has said. We challenge the very purposes of God in our lives, but we must keep on going. God is there all the time.

> **WE CHALLENGE THE VERY PURPOSES OF GOD IN OUR LIVES, BUT WE MUST KEEP ON GOING. GOD IS THERE ALL THE TIME.**

As we drove out of the Soviet Union across the border, I saw the other confiscated vehicles, most of which I recognized. I was quite ecstatic and, to say the least, relieved to be driving our van into freedom. I looked over, and to my surprise and bewilderment, my wife Alta was sitting in the seat next to me weeping. I thought she might have just been breaking from the horrendously overwhelming experience we had just been through. When I inquired what was wrong, I was totally taken aback by her response.

"We can never come back again" she sobbed. I could not believe what I was hearing.

My response was unreservedly: "What? That's the least of my worries! Let's get out of this hell hole! Never mind about coming back!" I think this was a fairly natural response.

Yet, unexpectedly, came forceful thoughts into my very innermost being. Though it was like a thought I could have formulated myself—an idea of some kind—it was not. Why not? Because first of all, it was the farthest thing from my natural mind and thoughts. I was not even thinking in that direction or much of anything except to get out of there as fast and as far as I could. However, over the years, I've learned it had to be God. I am trying to describe it to make it as clear and understandable to you as possible. I could easily have said, "And I heard the voice of God saying," but this may lead you to some preconceived idea of what that should sound like. So instead, I will try break it down as simply as I can. It might help you to understand that you may be hearing God much easier and more often than you ever thought you possibly could.

You see, if God has a purpose for your life and there is direction from Him in all of this—we need to hear it; we need to listen and talk about it with Him. This leads to the conversations we have with Him and the fellowship and communion that follow as a result. It can be information and direction, it can be comfort and reassurance, it can be a challenge, or it could be just a nice talk with Jesus. It helps so much to have a good conversation with

SENT...

Him. He has so much to say, and we have much we need to hear! I will elaborate more on this later and illustrate what I mean in order to encourage you in what you are already experiencing. I hope it gives you some guidance and reassurance to build your relationship with your Lord and Master by listening to what He has to say to you.

GOD HAS SO MUCH TO SAY, AND WE HAVE MUCH WE NEED TO HEAR!

So, what and how did I hear God speak to me? I will endeavor to explain. It was like a deep impression right in the center of my being which formed into words and registered in my mind. The thoughts did not come from my intellect but deeper. They came to my mind in the following words:

> *Don't worry about what has just happened. One day, I will open the door again. When I do it, I will do it in such a great way, you will know without a doubt it was My hand that did it!*

These words registered in a way I will never forget. Yet I write these things down daily because it is a good practice, not only for information but to spark a "conversation" with God. This is the instruction given in Habakkuk 2:1:

> *I will stand on my guard post and station myself on the rampart; And I will keep watch to see what He will speak to me, And how I may reply when I am reproved. Then the Lord answered me and said, "Record the vision and inscribe it on tablets, that the one who reads it may run. For the vision is yet for the appointed time; It hastens*

toward the goal and it will not fail. Though it tarries, wait for it; For it will certainly come, it will not delay."

It is of utmost importance to pay attention to accurately discern what God is saying. I cannot begin to emphasize this enough. It leads us not only to our future but in our daily walk, in the purposes of each day for which we were born. Jesus spent time listening to His Father. The following verses show us, I think, what Jesus's prayer life mostly consisted of:

- John 5:19: "Therefore Jesus answered and was saying to them, 'Truly, truly, I say to you, the Son can do nothing of Himself, unless it is something He sees the Father doing; for whatever the Father does, these things the Son also does in like manner.'"
- John 8:26-28: "I have many things to speak and to judge concerning you, but He who sent Me is true; and the things which I heard from Him, these I say to the world." They did not realize that He had been speaking to them about the Father. So Jesus said, "When you lift up the Son of Man, then you will know that I am He, and I do nothing on My own, but I say these things as the Father instructed Me."
- John 12:49: "For I did not speak on My own initiative, but the Father Himself who sent Me has given Me a commandment as to what to say and what to speak."
- John 14:31: "That the world may know that I love the Father, I do exactly as the Father commanded Me. Get up, let us go from here."

At that moment, as we left the Soviet Union, though I was not looking for it, I needed to hear and get a different perspective on the matter. I took the word I had received and shared that one day,

SENT...

God would open the door once again in the Soviet Union. With great enthusiasm, I would preach in the Estonian communities in Stockholm and Toronto telling of my experiences and saying that God would open the door once again for the people of Estonia and those in our country would be free again!

The old Estonians, especially those who had suffered so much and escaped with their lives the same time my parents did at the end of World War II in 1944, had long lost hope of ever seeing their homeland again and would listen quietly and seriously. The old men would come to me after service, pat me gently on the shoulder, and in their low, steady, and serious voices, share their opinions: "Young man, that is a really nice story, but we are sorry to say—we will never see that day. It will never happen." I understood. But, I had heard the voice of God. He had spoken, and so I kept these things in my heart, preached on, and believed He was in control of it all and waited for the day.

Many of my plans for the future in pastoring in Canada were fueled by the fact that, one day, God would open the door again, and I would return to Estonia. I remember being interviewed by the church board who asked about my plans and intentions. I told them I would be happy to be their pastor, but there would be a day I would leave when the time was right and go back to Estonia. They smiled politely, and that seemed to be the end of the matter for them. Years passed, and then it happened. One morning, I was driving to my church office and all of a sudden, I felt as if I were driving in Estonia. It was a strange feeling as I knew I was in Canada, approaching Fredericton (the capital of New Brunswick) where I had pastored for a little over eleven years. Then came the voice of God again, down deep in my Spirit.

Like I said, I had learned to identify His voice daily in my life. I would keep a journal and write down our conversations. But I would say there are different degrees of and different "velocities" to what God is saying. For example, there are the gentle talks, cautions, corrections, affirmations, and encouragements. Then there are times His voice hits you like a ton of bricks! Wham! There it is, and there is nothing more to say about it—it is so complete, so final, and so full of energy. It is like a bolt of lightning straight out of heaven, striking the very depths of my soul, just like I experienced at the border some eleven years earlier. It was not the only time this happened but one of the many, and here it was again: *You have not got a whole lot of time. Whatever you need to get ready, do it quickly because soon you will be leaving.*

GOD'S VOICE IS LIKE A BOLT OF LIGHTNING STRAIGHT OUT OF HEAVEN!

Now, there are times you know what He is saying even if it takes you by surprise. This took me by surprise, but I knew it was not a warning to get ready for my death. I just knew it was one thing—it would be time to move back to Estonia soon, and things would begin to happen.

I drove to the church office and called my assistant, Pastor Verner Drost, into the office and directly asked him the question: "Verner, if I left, would you be ready to pastor this church?"

Wide-eyed, he looked at me and said: "No, indeed not."

I responded: "Well, in that case, hurry up, and get ready because I am leaving soon."

SENT...

Soon after that, I passed the pastorate of the church over to Verner, worked with him for a year after that, and he remains there until this day while I moved back to Estonia where I have been ever since. Why do I say all of this? It is because God has a plan. What He spoke to me on the Moldavian border in the then Soviet Union under extremely difficult circumstances was fulfilled fourteen years later just as God said it would be. I was ready for that move and did not have to make it happen—I simply fit into what His plan was to begin with. He just had to tell me enough to direct my heart and be ready. He did the rest, and I followed. Now, as we will further discuss and understand, following is not always easy in and of itself. But with the commission comes the support and all that is required. We will benefit as we walk in obedience.

If we are going to live our lives His way, we need to desperately see what He wants to tell us about them. If He says nothing, that is also fine. I have no doubt whatsoever that our Lord will tell us what He thinks we need to hear, when we need to hear it. This is called walking in faith and trust.

I could have thought of many other and better ways for this chapter of our lives to conclude, but we needed to trust the One who had "sent" us in the first place. The question that must be asked, then, is this: "Whose way?" In other words, under whose direction will I attempt to live out the purposes of my life? Hence, is it presenting my crafted and created ideals of how my life should be, for various reasons and purposes, deciding what should happen and when, and then presenting it as an option to God for His approval and blessing? You might even be tempted to try to convince God that it is a good idea for Him to adopt such a brilliantly fashioned and designed plan. In reality, you are, in fact, endeavoring to do it your way and desiring to move on doing your thing.

BY WHOSE CHOICE AND INITIATIVE?

Often, we talk about choosing Christ. "I have chosen Christ as my Lord and Master." It sounds good. But no, it is not the truth. In actuality, He has chosen *us*. I think we have it backwards:

"You have not chosen Me, but I have chosen you and I have appointed you [I have planted you], that you might go and bear fruit and keep on bearing, and that your fruit may be lasting [that it may remain, abide], so that whatever you ask the Father in My Name [as presenting all that I Am], He may give it to you." —John 15:16 (AMPC)

God is all-knowing and supreme in His knowledge of what, who, when, and where. He knew all about us, our every day, even before we were born or had any substance at all! The psalms put it nicely:

Even before there is a word on my tongue, Behold, Lord, You know it all. You have encircled me behind and in front, And placed Your hand upon me. Such knowledge is too wonderful for me; It is too high, I cannot comprehend it. . . . Your eyes have seen my formless substance; And in Your book were written All the days that were ordained for me, When as yet there was not one of them.
—Psalms 139:4-6, 16

Does not the Bible say about Jeremiah, "Before I formed you in the womb I knew you, and before you were born I consecrated you; I have appointed you as a prophet to the nations" (Jeremiah 1:5)? Indeed, that was the prophet, but God knows you just as

SENT...

well. He knows us all and has designed and tailored your life for you. This prophet had a specific job, calling, and purpose. You have a purpose, specifically designed for you that is the best possibility according to the divine purpose of God for your life. In fact, He knew you before the world was formed:

> *Just as He chose us in Him before the foundation of the world, that we would be holy and blameless before Him. In love He predestined us to adoption as sons and daughters through Jesus Christ to Himself, according to the good pleasure of His will.* — Ephesians 1:4-5

And Romans 8:28 says, "And we know that God causes all things to work together for good to those who love God, to those who are called according to His purpose." Here we have it—"according to His purpose." That's the God element. You are unique in His design and purpose which is for you and you alone!

> **YOU ARE UNIQUE IN HIS DESIGN AND PURPOSE WHICH IS FOR YOU AND YOU ALONE!**

In the very same manner as I have described here, through a series of God's unusual directions, I was led to a very conservative, historical Pentecostal church. Soon, with a heart full of fire and passion, we all moved forward with the charismatic revival of that time, and amid opposition, together with challenges of every nature, we built and moved into what became known as Smythe Street Cathedral—one of the leading churches of the Fredericton and Eastern Provinces of Canada. God directed us:

> *For those whom He foreknew, He also predestined to become conformed to the image of His Son, so that He*

would be the firstborn among many brethren; and these whom He predestined, He also called; and these whom He called, He also justified; and these whom He justified, He also glorified. What then shall we say to these things? If God is for us, who is against us? —Romans 8:29-31

The verses above show one thing: God makes the choice. God takes the initiative! He has done this since before time began through His foreknowledge. Therefore the success of the ministry while in Fredericton was His by His initiative. I was simply the instrument in submission to Him, doing His will! In this scripture we can clearly see His choices and initiative. How many personal pronouns are in these verses alone? Count them. Over and over, we can tally a multitude of "He" and "His" pronouns!

In all the various things I moved on to—though I calculated and planned—I experienced God's orchestrations whether I was serving as a volunteer chaplain in the local hospital or later as the first non-Anglican chaplain of the Province of New Brunswick Legislative Assembly. I could see the divine leading and direction of God in it all. I sensed the same as I served on the leadership board and missionary council and was also the Atlantic district director of Apostolic Church of Pentecost of Canada. In the same manner as I served in Canada I knew the day would arrive, and so it did, when I would return to Estonia as the Iron Curtain began to crumble.

The whole Bible is the story of God's initiative on behalf of mankind. Before we knew who, how, or when, and before we even knew to ask or take a step toward God, He was in action, knowing us and working on our behalf. What a wonderful thing! Even before we knew how to begin to move toward God, the initiative

SENT...

of God was in motion on our behalf as described so uniquely in Romans 5:6 (AMPC): "While we were yet in weakness [powerless to help ourselves], at the fitting time, Christ died for (in behalf of) the ungodly."

Even while we were doing our thing to the extent of being enemies of God, what was God doing? Romans 5:10 says, "For if while we were enemies we were reconciled to God through the death of His Son, much more, having been reconciled, we shall be saved by His life"

God has taken the initiative because He is a God of love He loves mankind. He wants mankind to have the best and live successfully that we might live our lives to our absolute fullest potential. He wants and has prepared all of this for us! According to 1 John 4:10 (AMPC) says, "*In this is love*: not that we loved God, but that *He loved us* and sent His Son to be the propitiation (the atoning sacrifice) for our sins." Notice that I've emphasized by italicizing "In this is love" and "He loved us." We must see how those words relate to each other.

This is the initiative of God—the sovereignty of God at work. It is the Holy God of this universe in action! It was this kind of preparation that moved us into the Soviet Union with our two teenage children, in spite of the fact I had been barred for life, with two other Estonian families who had grown up in Sweden/Canada: the Allan Laur family and the Harry Leesment family from Australia. A trio of us, from various organizations like the Assemblies of Canada, Assemblies of God in Australia, and the Apostolic Church of Pentecost of Canada (where I worked), set up a national church—the Estonian Christian Pentecostal Church.

It was a move that started several dozen churches, a prison ministry, a missions outreach, a radio station, a Bible school, and a humanitarian network throughout the country over a short few years. We worked hand in hand with other Christians and churches, all with great historical changes in the country and challenges in our personal lives and families. Today, Allan and his wife Rael have passed on from this life; Harry and Jackie and their family are back in Australia. Alta and I remain.

It may come as a bit of a surprise to us, but whether we realize it or not, we do not even belong to ourselves. This is not a popular message in the age of "rights," but it is so true. First Corinthians 6:19 reminds us, "Or do you not know that your body is a temple of the Holy Spirit who is in you, whom you have from God, and that you are not your own?"

You are not your own! Very sobering when we think about the way we would want to do things, love things, and arrange our own lives and decisions. We so often do so much according to what suits us, even good things, because we think we have the "right" to do so, or have the "right" to have what we want. This requires some very serious thinking because "you have been bought with a price: therefore glorify God in your body" (1 Corinthians 6:20).

DESTINY FOR YOU DOES NOT NOR DID IT EVER JUST HAPPEN.

Again, we come face-to-face with the claims of our destiny. Destiny for you does not nor did it ever just happen. First, there was the initiative of God from the beginning of all time. Then came evil that stole all of our God-given destiny from us and

SENT...

threw mankind into what seemed like endless chaos, pain, and suffering—a far cry from what God had intended. This came by the choice of man and decisions that he made starting in the garden of Eden and has made ever since. More often than not, man has walked below what God intended for him. To prey on man's weaknesses, Satan the thief came to "steal and kill and destroy," but Jesus came so that "they may have life, and have *it* abundantly" (John 10:10).

God's unwavering initiative swings into a full counterattack to bring us back to our fullest potential: abundant life. What a contrast! But it comes with an unrelenting price. He buys us back with His Son's life. His life for yours! "For God so loved the world, that He gave His only begotten Son, that whoever believes in Him shall not perish, but have eternal life" (John 3:16).

That is why we are not our own; we have been "bought with a price," according to 1 Corinthians 6:20 (NIV). Indeed, it was a high price to pay. Could there have been a higher price? I believe it was the ultimate price; there was none other to surpass or even come close to it.

Many of us understand only one aspect of this purchase. We feel we were bought to be free from sin, free to go to heaven, and free to start all over again. While all of these aspects of the purchase are true, they are but a limited portion of the whole picture. We were purchased, so we would, once again, belong to Him and be brought back to Him who first owned us. He would now bring us back into what He wanted and intended for us in the very beginning. He has a plan and this plan is God's thing—His plan and destiny for us, not our thing or our way. The Bible is full of this. Just look at the previously marked scripture from John

10:10 where Jesus claims His coming will enable us to enjoy life and have it in abundance!

As just mentioned, it is quite a different story from what Satan wants. In the same verse that describes abundant life (John 10:10), we find he wants to bait us by coming "in order to steal and kill and destroy."

Let's again revisit Christ's side of this great picture:

For you know the grace of our Lord Jesus Christ, that though He was rich, yet for your sake He became poor, so that you through His poverty might become rich."
—*2 Corinthians 8:9*

Just think of it! What a powerful exchange! Can we grasp our end of this transition? Though it makes no sense to the human mind and our way of calculating things, the facts are there. Romans 5:55 (AMP) backs this up: "Such hope [in God's promises] never disappoints us, because God's love has been *abundantly* poured out within our hearts through the Holy Spirit who was given to us."

There was nothing cheap about this, nothing done sparingly, but it was "abundantly poured out." Then, this is how we are to "abundantly" receive it also!

The following verses expound on an unbelievable fact:

But the free gift [of God] is not like the trespass [because the gift of grace overwhelms the fall of man]. For if many died by one man's trespass [Adam's sin], much more [abundantly] did God's grace and the gift [that comes] by the grace of the one Man, Jesus Christ, overflow to [benefit] the many. —*Romans 5:15 (AMP)*

SENT...

Paul himself expressed this while standing in front of the council of Areopagus in Athens. He declared:

> "That they would seek God, if perhaps they might grope for Him and find Him, though He is not far from each one of us; for in Him we live and move and exist, as even some of your own poets have said, 'For we also are His children.'" —Acts 17:27-28

Then, Paul so clearly declared this to the Romans 6:4-5:

> Therefore we have been buried with Him through baptism into death, so that as Christ was raised from the dead through the glory of the Father, so we too might walk in newness of life. For if we have become united with Him in the likeness of His death, certainly we shall also be in the likeness of His resurrection.

This new life is His resurrection life in us and us in Him:

> Now if we have died with Christ, we believe that we shall also live with Him, knowing that Christ, having been raised from the dead, is never to die again; death no longer is master over Him. For the death that He died, He died to sin once for all; but the life that He lives, He lives to God. Even so consider yourselves to be dead to sin, but alive to God in Christ Jesus. —Romans 6:8-11

Once again, Paul declares with excitement the same to the Galatians, as if he did not even have a life of his own:

> I have been crucified with Christ; and it is no longer I who live, but Christ lives in me; and the life which I now live in the flesh I live by faith in the Son of God, who loved me and gave Himself up for me. —Galatians 2:20

You Were Born for and With a Purpose!

What is this now that brings us to a place where He is "not far from each one of us," where "in Him we live and move and exist," where we walk in "newness of life," where we "live with Him," where we are "alive to God," and where "it is no longer I who live, but Christ lives in me?"

> **SO OFTEN, WE TALK ABOUT WHAT WE WERE SAVED FROM. PAUL TALKS ABOUT THE ABUNDANCE OF WHAT CHRIST HAS PURCHASED US INTO!**

What is he talking about here? This puts a whole new dimension to things and experiences when it comes to salvation and redemption. So often, we talk about what we were saved *from*. Here, He talks about the abundance of what Christ has purchased us *into*! These scriptures are just the tip of the iceberg. Wow, we would need an entire book by itself on this very subject alone!

Once we get the idea of what the word "Sent" in the title of this book might mean and ask ourselves, "Whose way?" we will choose, we will begin to realize there is something really great in this! We really were born with and for a purpose! It is not what you can produce but what He has produced for you that is waiting to happen. It is your destiny—it is His way for you! You really are Sent by Him to achieve the best there is for you—His purpose!

You were indisputably born with a divine purpose! You have an exclusive, irreplaceable God-given destiny designed for you!

SENT...

YOU WERE INDISPUTABLY BORN WITH A DIVINE PURPOSE! YOU HAVE AN EXCLUSIVE, IRREPLACEABLE GOD-GIVEN DESTINY DESIGNED FOR YOU!

How do I become convinced of this truth? How did it become a practical reality for me? How do I discover this personally, for my family, my work, my vocation, my calling, my church, and my country? What we have discussed in this chapter is only one aspect of the entire picture, so to answer these questions, we must move on to another important and pivotal aspect of this discussion and subject.

We must begin to understand where we are right now in this process and what we are to do in order to move forward. We will do that next.

CHAPTER 3

MARCHING ORDERS

IN THE SAME WAY

At the beginning of this book, I pointed out and want to repeat that I want to zero in on one important aspect of what I discovered during my reading of what Jesus said and taught in John 20:21. Let's look at how different translations present it:

- King James Version (KJV): " Then said Jesus to them again, Peace be unto you: as my Father hath sent me, even so send I you."
- New American Standard Bible (NASB): "So Jesus said to them again, 'Peace be with you; as the Father has sent Me, I also send you.'"
- New International Version (NIV): "Again Jesus said, 'Peace be with you! As the Father has sent me, I am sending you.'"

SENT...

- Young's Literal Translation (YLT): "Jesus, therefore, said to them again, 'Peace to you; according as the Father hath sent me, I also send you.'"
- J. B. Phillips New Testament (PHILLIPS): "Jesus said to them again, 'Yes, peace be with you! Just as the Father sent me, so I am now going to send you.'"
- Easy-to-Read Version (ERV): "Then Jesus said again, 'Peace be with you. It was the Father who sent me, and I am now sending you in the same way.'"

The list can go on and on, but no matter what version you may be using, there is no doubt as to the clear meaning of the text. Jesus is saying this in a comparative way which significantly changes its importance and relates it to us in a very special and unique way.

I would draw your attention to the small words "as," "even so," and the "same way," in Jesus's words. If Jesus had said, "I was sent by the Father," and now "I am sending you," these words of Jesus would not have had as much impact and implication. "As" and "even so" change everything. What He is really saying cannot be taken any other way except: "It was the Father who sent me, and I am now sending you in the same way" (John 20:21, ERV).

Comparatively speaking, we are sent in the same way He was sent. Found in an entirely different setting, another powerful prayer—The High Priestly Prayer—to the Father is said by Jesus in John 17. He emphasizes the fact that He was "sent" of the Father and is sending out His disciples. He repeats it six times in this prayer alone:

- verse 3: "And this is eternal life, that they may know You, the only true God, and Jesus Christ whom You have sent."

- verse 8: "The words which You gave Me I have given to them; and they received them and truly understood that I came forth from You, and they believed that You sent Me."
- verse 18: "Just as You sent Me into the world, I also sent them into the world."
- verse 23: "That they may be perfected in unity, so that the world may know that You sent Me."
- verse 25: "Righteous Father, although the world has not known You, yet I have known You; and these have known that You sent Me."

This supportively underlines the whole subject of what we examine in this book. Furthermore, in the same chapter and context, He emphasizes His accomplished work in verse 4 "which You have given Me to do." In other words, Jesus was sent to do a specific work which the Father had given him to do. Then, in the middle of this prayer, an unusual statement emerges in verse 18: "Just as You sent Me into the world, I also sent them into the world." The Passion Translation expresses it as: "*I have commissioned them* to represent me *just as you commissioned me* to represent you." The wording matches John 20:21.

> **THERE IS NO DOUBT ABOUT IT. WE ARE SENT BY JESUS HIMSELF AS HE WAS SENT BY HIS FATHER.**

There is no doubt about it. We are *sent* by Jesus Himself as He was *sent* by His Father. This is not an isolated statement taken out of context in the writing of this book. It is fully supported by the whole concept of the principle of Jesus's ministry in relation to the

SENT...

Father, His commission, us, the world around us, and our purpose in it. We will refer to this principle as we continue our study.

If you and I want to know how we are sent by Jesus, then it would be extremely wise and important for us to pay close attention to how Jesus was sent by His Father and compare notes. If so, exactly by whom are "we sent?" That is exactly what I set out to discover for myself from the Scriptures and the life of Jesus. We have the gospels for reference as we determine exactly by whom and how we are sent.

BLESS ME ON MY MISSION

I have heard it all my life about the fact that Jesus has sent us—the "Go ye" part. For example, in one of many passages in the Gospels, Mark 16:15 (KJV) says, "And he said unto them, Go ye into all the world, and preach the gospel to every creature."

Although I heard these phrases for many years, they became just a familiar slogan that I took for granted. Also, I'm afraid we all have read into this statement using our own preconceived ideas and perhaps those of someone else. This can happen with scriptures we are often familiar with. I am afraid I have done so. In obedience, I have done the "Go ye" with this attitude, more or less: "Here I go, Lord. I am on a mission, and now I want or need Your blessing upon what I am setting out to do."

The first realization we must face is that Jesus says our sending must happen His way and on His terms. We are not volunteers. We neither give ourselves, nor do we offer ourselves! This was never any clearer to me than when I experienced God speak to my heart.

Leadership was now well-established; in fact, there was a third generation of leaders emerging in the national Estonian

Christian Pentecostal Church. I felt I had been obedient to God when coming to the country to raise up leadership and let them carry on yet support them as a mentor and father in the work.

Now, once again, God spoke to my spirit very clearly. I was taken aback at what I heard: *You have not even touched Estonia until you reach those who are in the deepest of darkness and despair!* I had no idea who these people might be. I had preached on the streets, in the prisons, and in churches all over the country. Yet, God was saying I had not yet even touched the country. I was puzzled, and when I asked who these people might be, I received no answer.

> **I HAD PREACHED ON THE STREETS, IN THE PRISONS, AND IN CHURCHES ALL OVER ESTONIA. YET, GOD WAS SAYING I HAD NOT YET EVEN TOUCHED THE COUNTRY.**

I looked for a place where I might help these particular people, whoever they may be. I was not sure who, yet I had in mind to perhaps begin building some type of a haven—a shelter of some kind where they may live and be safe. It was not clear to me what exactly I needed to do, but I continued to move on by the constant tug of what I sensed the Holy Spirit was saying in my heart and what I was sure God had spoken to me.

Both my sons loved to party. They drank heavily and pursued having a good time. To me, they seemed to have little, if any, interest in what I was doing in the church in Estonia. Although I would enjoy their company and being with them, they lived lives totally other than what I knew or how I raised them. They

SENT...

would laugh and tell me of their parties—tales that would make me angry and other times just discouraged. I would often think, *Why should I be doing what I am doing, being faithful to what I feel is the will and purpose of God in my life and at the same time be unable to reach my own sons?* In anguish, I wrestled with these thoughts until one day, quite unexpectedly, God spoke to me very specifically. *Don't try to change them—simply love them as much as you can and in whatever way you deem best. Spend time with them.*

I understood well that at this stage of things, there was little I could do to teach them anything I thought was necessary, let alone require or demand some kind of change. They had grown up in the church and in a Christian home and had heard it all. I wondered how I might be obedient to what I felt God's instructions were. I finally decided to take my son Andrew with me as I traveled and spoke at various surrounding churches during my visits to Canada, presenting the missions work overseas. This would give us a good opportunity to spend time with each other and enjoy traveling together.

I figured there was little chance he would want to be in church, let alone listen to me speak on the work of missions and challenge people to get involved. So in light of this, I made a suggestion while driving home from a meeting one night in St. Stephen back to Fredericton: "I know you don't want to be in church. Perhaps you prefer to take a stroll up the street or whatever and then meet up again after the service. I would not be offended if you would prefer this."

There was a pause and a moment of silence. I was not expecting what came next. I kept driving, almost spellbound, when Andrew quite deliberately took a long breath and replied: "Dad, anyone can destroy their life like I am doing. But only a few can do what you are doing—I would rather do what you are doing!"

I was stunned. I did not dare open my mouth for fear I would ruin the moment. Finally, I simply replied: "In that case, I guess you will have to make a decision," upon which, Andrew replied: "Dad, you're the expert, tell me what I have to do." I had not heard such a statement coming from my son for as long as I could remember. I was at a total loss for words. This was such an unexpected change of events. It took me by full surprise. In short, we pulled the car to the side of the road and there, Andrew submitted his life to Christ. It was one of those "God moments." My heart is moved every time at the very memory of it.

Andrew claimed in his heart a call from God to work with those who had the same problem he had: addiction. He went on to Bible school and then to study and train in the field of addictions with Frank Costantino and the Bridges of America in Orlando, Florida, and finally, with Mickey Evans and Hugh Murrow at Dunklin Memorial Rehab Center near Okeechobee, Florida.

Afterward, Andrew came back to Estonia, and together, with one purpose and call, we founded on my grandfather's lands the Village of Hope. Through my son, God showed me who He was referring to when he said I would help those "in the deepest of darkness and despair!" They were those suffering chemical addiction—the alcoholic and the drug addict.

You see, it was never *my* idea to enter this type of ministry. It was never *my* choice. I did not understand anything about what it would require and in my opinion, was the least qualified for the job. I feel a bit of underlying guilt confessing this, but it was the last thing on earth I really planned to do. I had worked with

SENT...

people in prisons and had a heart to help them, and I see how it was the plan of God in my life. Ironically though, I was blind to the direct connection between addiction and most prisoners at the time. I saw prison ministry as part of our obligation as a church, yet for me to directly help the alcoholic was a mystery, other than to get him saved and in church.

The addict felt like someone "spooky" behind the corner or down an alleyway I did not want to meet or even try to understand. It was not my thing. I say this because I want to make a point. On top of the fact that I was not qualified, I had no compassion to help these people. I am sorry to say this but yet that is the way it was. This has since all changed—not by some emotional eye-opener or heart-wrenching story of compassion. It came one step at a time up to the point where I was at a place to listen. Then came my "marching orders" which left nothing but obedience. I understood obedience, and I knew what I had to do.

> **WE HAVE ALL KINDS OF REASONS WHY THINGS ARE NOT POSSIBLE, WHY IT CAN'T BE DONE, OR WHY SOMEONE ELSE WOULD BE BETTER QUALIFIED TO DO IT. BUT WHO KNOWS BETTER THAN HE WHO SENDS?**

It is amazing how things began to work out when we are ready to obey Him. We have all kinds of reasons why things are not possible, why it can't be done, or why someone else would be better qualified. But who knows better than He who sends? He has the plan in place, knows what must be done, and even knows the results before we begin. In the limitations of our knowledge,

Marching Orders

so often, we do not even know where or how to begin, but He will even look after that! All Christ looks for is the obedient attitude and starts with us where we are, leading us one step at a time as we dare to believe and trust in Him who sends.

The Bible is full of these examples. Who sent Abraham? Who voted for Moses? Who commissioned Samuel to go and anoint the shepherd boy David as a future king? The accounts go on and on until the very day Jesus appointed His disciples and gave them their marching orders:

Now as Jesus was walking by the Sea of Galilee, He saw two brothers, Simon, who was called Peter, and his brother Andrew, casting a net into the sea; for they were fishermen. And He said to them, "Follow Me, and I will make you fishers of men." Immediately they left their nets and followed Him. —Matthew 4:18-20

What qualifications did these men have to become apostles? Of all people, what qualified Peter to become the founding apostle of Christ's church here on earth? What credentials did any of them have to show for the task of responding to the call of Christ? What applications did they fill out, and what references did they give? Others saw these things accurately. Acts 4:13 describes other people's responses to the disciples: "Now as they observed the confidence of Peter and John and understood that they were uneducated and untrained men, they were amazed, and began to recognize them as having been with Jesus."

However, Paul said it quite plainly when he described such worldly wisdom:

Where is the wise person? Where is the scribe? Where is the debater of this age? Has God not made foolish

SENT...

the wisdom of the world? For since in the wisdom of God the world through its wisdom did not come to know God, God was well-pleased through the foolishness of the message preached to save those who believe. For indeed Jews ask for signs and Greeks search for wisdom; but we preach Christ crucified, to the Jews a stumbling block and to Gentiles foolishness, but to those who are the called, both Jews and Greeks, Christ the power of God and the wisdom of God. For the foolishness of God is wiser than mankind, and the weakness of God is stronger than mankind.

For consider your calling, brothers and sisters, that there were not many wise according to the flesh, not many mighty, not many noble; but God has chosen the foolish things of the world to shame the wise, and God has chosen the weak things of the world to shame the things which are strong, and the insignificant things of the world and the despised God has chosen, the things that are not, so that He may nullify the things that are, so that no human may boast before God. But it is due to Him that you are in Christ Jesus, who became to us wisdom from God, and righteousness and sanctification, and redemption, so that, just as it is written, "LET HIM WHO BOASTS, BOAST IN THE LORD."
—1 Corinthians 1:20-31

Now, not for a moment am I playing down education, study, and using our ability to learn and develop. But let these be the results of the divine commission of Christ, sending us to do the things we are not qualified to do. How quickly we slip into the methods of the world, knowledge, and academic achievements to qualify us in making an application before God that He should actually choose us and send us on that basis.

> **HOW QUICKLY WE SLIP INTO THE METHODS OF THE WORLD, KNOWLEDGE, AND ACADEMIC ACHIEVEMENTS TO QUALIFY US IN MAKING AN APPLICATION BEFORE GOD THAT HE SHOULD ACTUALLY CHOOSE US AND SEND US ON THAT BASIS.**

The man who wrote the passage above was the same one who was intercepted from heaven on the road to Damascus by Jesus, struck blind, and then led to a disciple named Ananias who was also instructed in a vision to go pray for Paul, known as Saul at that time. Ananias immediately reasoned with the Lord, informing Him of who Saul really was and that this was a bit unreasonable. The whole story can be found in Acts 9.

It sounds like us quite often, does it not? God asks us to do something that we cannot understand and that we feel very unqualified for, and we immediately begin to explain and inform God why this is not such a good idea. The Lord here gives no alternative. In Acts 9:15, we hear the Lord's response to Ananias:

> *"Go, for he is a chosen instrument of Mine, to bear My name before the Gentiles and kings and the sons of Israel; for I will show him how much he must suffer for My name's sake."*

You see, it is His plan—He has it all lined up under His conditions. He knew exactly what His intensions were for Saul. This is

SENT...

the eternally knowledgeable God who runs the universe and is qualified far beyond any one of us could ever be.

What was left for Saul? What was left for Ananias? Keep reading: *So Ananias departed and entered the house, and after laying his hands on him said, "Brother Saul, the Lord Jesus, who appeared to you on the road by which you were coming, has sent me so that you may regain your sight and be filled with the Holy Spirit." And immediately there fell from his eyes something like scales, and he regained his sight, and he got up and was baptized; and he took food and was strengthened. —Acts 9:17-19*

The only thing left for Ananias was obedience. Because God was the One arranging, calling, and sending, He also had the last word. Ananias did the only smart thing he could do—obey. It took powerful persuasion to do it, but the direction came from the Lord.

What a powerful illustration of the sovereign commission of God. Reading the whole chapter of Acts 9 gives a clear reason why the results were there—why it all happened. There were no instructions to God from Saul; there were none from Ananias. There were no long prayers to get God moving. There were no criteria of accomplishment or qualifications; there was simply the call to submit and obey the sovereign will and purpose of God which was already in full swing.

> **THERE WERE NO CRITERIA OF ACCOMPLISHMENT OR QUALIFICATIONS; THERE WAS SIMPLY THE CALL TO SUBMIT AND OBEY THE SOVEREIGN WILL AND PURPOSE OF GOD WHICH WAS ALREADY IN FULL SWING.**

Paul took another entire chapter to explain the spiritual depth of this whole principle. It is well worth noting:

And when I came to you, brothers and sisters, I did not come as someone superior in speaking ability or wisdom, as I proclaimed to you the testimony of God. For I determined to know nothing among you except Jesus Christ, and Him crucified. I also was with you in weakness and in fear and in much trembling, and my message and my preaching were not in persuasive words of wisdom, but in demonstration of the Spirit and of power, so that your faith would not rest on the wisdom of mankind, but on the power of God.

Yet we do speak wisdom among those who are mature; a wisdom, however, not of this age nor of the rulers of this age, who are passing away; but we speak God's wisdom in a mystery, the hidden wisdom which God predestined before the ages to our glory; the wisdom which none of the rulers of this age has understood; for if they had understood it, they would not have crucified the Lord of glory; but just as it is written, "Things which eye has not seen and ear has not heard, And which have not entered the human heart, All that God has prepared for those who love Him."

SENT...

For to us God revealed them through the Spirit; for the Spirit searches all things, even the depths of God. For who among men knows the thoughts of a person except the spirit of the person that is in him? So also the thoughts of God no one knows, except the Spirit of God. Now we have not received the spirit of the world, but the Spirit who is from God, so that we may know the things freely given to us by God, We also speak these things, not in words taught by human wisdom, but in those taught by the Spirit, combining spiritual thoughts with spiritual words.

But a natural person does not accept the things of the Spirit of God, for they are foolishness to him; and he cannot understand them, because they are spiritually discerned. But the one who is spiritual discerns all things, yet he himself is discerned by no one. For who has known the mind of the Lord, that he will instruct Him? But we have the mind of Christ. —1 Corinthians 2

> **UNDERSTAND THAT THE CALL AND MARCHING ORDERS FROM THE VERY PLAN AND PURPOSE OF GOD ARE THE FOUNDATION OF THE QUALIFICATION.**

Understand that the call and marching orders from the very plan and purpose of God are the foundation of the qualification. It is not the qualification itself but the basis for it. We then work toward the qualifications because we have been given the call—the marching orders. Going back again to Matthew 4:19-20, Jesus gives specific marching orders: "And He said to them, 'Follow Me, and I will make you fishers of men.' Immediately they left their nets and followed Him."

There was the order:

1) Follow Me.

2) I will make you fishers of men.

Jesus did not say, "You are," but "I will make you." They did what was commanded in obedience when they immediately left their nets and followed Him. Were they perfect? Did they qualify in being fishers of men? No, not by a long shot! Yet they did the one thing they were required to do in order to walk down that road. They *immediately* followed Him. I like that word. Without hesitation, they obeyed and submitted. Though they didn't have the qualifications or even understand what it all meant—they did it on the spot! It was obedience to His command: "Follow Me."

Then came the process of submitting to being made into fishers of men. I do not think the fishermen had any idea what was ahead of them. We read about their preexisting lack of qualifications; it was a school of hard knocks! They had to endure lots of trials, had many doubts, and had to learn many things. But the call was there, marching orders were issued, and they obeyed. The training for qualification had started.

THE CALL WAS THERE, MARCHING ORDERS WERE ISSUED, AND THEY OBEYED.

The work God called me to do was not much different. I had now learned who the people He wanted me to help were. Then came the steps that followed. Little did I realize how God would begin to qualify me to fulfill His orders and make me a fisher of

SENT...

men and women in addiction. I qualified as I learned day after day, month in and month out, continuing year after year—my teacher was none other than my son Andrew!

It was no different than what Ananias had witnessed with Saul; the problem had taken a 180-degree turn and now had become the answer. Not only was this work totally unforeseen, but also the solution to it was the furthest thing expected. Today, I count it a privilege and honor to work together with my son Andrew in the ministry God has sent us to do. I always say this was never my idea and what I was least educated in. But because God loves those in addiction, He also taught me how to minister to them and above all—how to love them.

I had always said I love everyone. I'd say, "Sure, I love these people," but I found out I had a lot to learn about how to love them properly—genuinely love them. Like everything else, I learned. I hate what addiction had done and what it continues to cause: devastation, hurt, and family pain. I loathe the self-destruction of human life and the crippling effects not only for the addict, but the children, spouses, and grandparents. Yet, because Christ loved and commanded me to love also, I have learned to work with them and love them.

Since its genesis, the Village of Hope has received numerous recognitions and awards from the government, police, and local authorities for the work we have done. On February 22, 2013, on the eve of Estonian National Independence Ceremonies, I was awarded the Order of the Red Cross III Category for services rendered to the Estonian People by the Estonian President Indrek Ilves. On national television, President Ilves thanked me. And in front of a hall filled with distinguished people, all of a sudden, I heard the voice of God deep in my spirit: *Today, you have touched Estonia.*

I walked off the platform with a praise and satisfaction in my heart toward God because I knew it was never my idea, but many years earlier, I had only been obedient to that which I had been sent to do by Christ Himself! I had the deep satisfaction and gratification that comes from "obedience." You could not have paid me enough for that moment—the moment I heard His voice, knowing the success of what had happened was only because of Him.

My wife Alta and our son Andrew were present during the ceremony. I knew my wife had stood faithfully beside me, as always, both of us determined to do it together. I also knew Andrew had been obedient to the call of God on his life, and in sacrifice and determination, he had earned every bit of the honor that I earned. As many members of our team and family moved together in faith and obedience, the Order of the Red Cross was a victory and above all, a great honor to Christ our Lord and His kingdom.

Hundreds of addicts' lives continue to be touched and transformed, not only here in Estonia but also in Canada. Andrew presently lives with his family in Canada, and we lead the Village of Hope in New Brunswick and Estonia together. This has also brought into play a whole network of supporters, partners, businesses, associates, individuals, and churches from across Europe and North America who have all worked together to build the Village of Hope. To write the tales of God's provision in these cases would indeed require another book.

SENT...

TO WRITE THE TALES OF GOD'S PROVISION WOULD, INDEED, REQUIRE ANOTHER BOOK.

When we founded the Village of Hope, God specifically instructed us look for two hundred acres of land with a river going through the middle of it but to not pay more than ONE Canadian dollar for it! An elderly gentleman named Byron Phillips offered to show us his lands, of course, knowing neither the requirements nor the size. At first, Andrew and I did not even want to go look at it as it was not where we wanted it to be. Furthermore, we knew Byron to be a shrewd businessman, who, in our estimation, would want a lot of money for his lands. But God spoke to our hearts to go see the land, and when we saw the river flowing through the middle of it, we wondered, *Could this be it?* There was just one way to find out.

Over a bowl of soup at lunch, Andrew and I made the proposal. The first thing we asked him was, "Are there two hundred acres?" Byron thought about it and replied that he was sure there might be that or close to it. Then we did it: "Byron, would you consider giving us two hundred acres, both sides of the river, and we would not offer more than $1 for it?"

Byron leaned over and in a split second replied, "Without a hesitation!"

We thought he might have misunderstood, but upon clarifying our thoughts once again, Byron replied: "While you boys were down at the river, God spoke to me and told me that whatever you asked from me, I was to give it to you—I was waiting for you to ask!"

We found a Canadian dollar, framed it, and presented it to Byron as he sat in his rocking chair, leaned back with tears in his eyes, and said: "Isn't my God so good! Of all the land in this country, He would choose mine!" The surveyor measured the same lot of donated land which today is the Village of Hope in New Brunswick—exactly two hundred acres!

Since then and during the time of this writing, the Villages of Hope are beginning to be built in Finland. Just this year, in another miraculous story, a Village of Hope has been built in Cuba! And on top of it all, in Eston, Saskatchewan, we can tell another fabulous story of the overwhelmingly generous gift from the Apostolic Church of Pentecost of Canada and Eston College leadership, who helped us obtain an entire Bible school campus with facilities that hold two hundred students and staff—again, for the sum of ONLY $1!

It is a beautiful story of how God arranges things in His way and in His time. Just one year ago, we would have never even dreamed of such things happening. These are all things God has so uniquely arranged and "Sent" us to receive because there are thousands of those in addiction God has also "Sent" us to!

This, of course, does not eliminate the numerous challenges as we expand and grow, yet it goes on, one step at a time, and every step in and of itself is a story of the leading, guidance, and provision of Christ. Not a single day goes by that I do not personally consult, talk to, and have conversations with Jesus. They are both the most enjoyable times and also the most soul-searching times with questions and answers. After all, it is He who continues to direct, send, commission, and lead.

SENT...

NOT A SINGLE DAY GOES BY THAT I DO NOT PERSONALLY CONSULT, TALK TO, AND HAVE CONVERSATIONS WITH JESUS.... AFTER ALL, IT IS HE WHO CONTINUES TO DIRECT, SEND, COMMISSION, AND LEAD.

Do I hit the bull's-eye on every decision or every undertaking? No, I wish I could say that I do. However, one thing is for sure: it is not myself, our staff, or our organizational structure trying to accomplish something or planning some type of expansion, doing something, and then hoping Jesus is somewhere in the midst of our plans to help us, support us, and stand with us. It is one continual journey of challenges, victories, and adventures—together with Christ, planned by Him and lead by Him! We do it together, and I have a lot to learn each day from His Holy Spirit. The challenges I face will endure forever during this lifetime, but there is one thing I always understand and recognize again and again: it is neither my initiative nor my ideas that move me forward. He is my source, making me ever so conscious of Christ and dependent on Him. It's actually pretty exciting!

This, by far, is not my experience alone. I have related just a few illustrations of what I have experienced myself. You may have many similar experiences and tales to tell. I hope others are encouraged and learn the same. We are all different and all chosen, commissioned and sent by Christ Himself. Jesus very specifically says in John 15:16:

"You did not choose Me but I chose you, and appointed you that you would go and bear fruit, and that your fruit

would remain, so that whatever you ask of the Father in My name He may give to you."

We all, in one way or other, are appointed and sent to follow strict marching orders! If that term sounds a bit too militant, then try seeing it from the angle of being under divine command. Even in the military, a command or commission is not itself the end goal. There is a purpose to achieve but with a much greater meaning—a divine purpose. The appointment does not just stand isolated; rather, it is connected to a specific assignment as stated in John 15:16, "That you would go and bear fruit, and that your fruit would remain."

Those of us who think we have so graciously volunteered or done God some super favor by giving ourselves to Christ must face what the Bible says. I mentioned it earlier, but I'll mention it again. We don't even belong to ourselves—we belong to Him! We are rightfully His to begin with!

> **DID IT EVER OCCUR TO US THAT IN DOING IT OUR WAY, WE ARE ACTUALLY, IN FACT, SELLING OURSELVES SHORT?**

We will deal with this question later, but at this point, you may feel that I am losing my own will and purpose or that I would lose my quality of life and its purpose. How can I just give up so much? Do we really gain much more with our own accomplishments? By giving them up, do we actually lose out? Perhaps we need to see what really brings to us to the point of losing it all or submitting to God's commands! Did it ever occur to us that in

SENT...

doing it our way, we are actually, in fact, selling ourselves short? Did not Jesus Himself say:

> *I tell you the truth, unless a kernel of wheat is planted in the soil and dies, it remains alone. But its death will produce many new kernels—a plentiful harvest of new lives. Those who love their life in this world will lose it. Those who care nothing for their life in this world will keep it for eternity.* —John 12:24-25 (NLT)

Did Jesus lose in life with a submissive attitude toward his Father? Once again, let's look at the life of Jesus. Remember how the Father sent Him, so He sends us? Our being sent is a parallel to Jesus being sent by the Father. Therefore, we need to see how Jesus responded to the Father when He was sent so that we learn how we should respond in surrendering ourselves to Jesus.

> **WE NEED TO SEE HOW JESUS RESPONDED TO THE FATHER WHEN HE WAS SENT SO THAT WE LEARN HOW WE SHOULD RESPOND IN SURRENDERING OURSELVES TO JESUS.**

Let's start with some simple facts, which we will elaborate on later. The first fact is that Jesus did not give Himself to the Father anywhere in the Bible. He only submitted to the Father to whom He belonged in the first place and did His will. He belonged to the Father. He was born of the Father.

In my natural birth, I was born to my parents. Therefore, I belonged to them. I am my mother's child and my father's son! It comes with my birth! That is why we are to honor our parents and obey them. It is the same as the biblical principle outlined in Ephesians 6:1-3:

> Children, obey your parents in the Lord, for this is right. Honor your father and mother (which is the first commandment with a promise), so that it may turn out well for you, and that you may live long on the earth.

Jesus was born of His Father:

> And the angel answered and said unto her, "The Holy Ghost shall come upon thee, and the power of the Highest shall overshadow thee: therefore also that holy thing which shall be born of thee shall be called the Son of God." —Luke 1:35

In our spiritual birth, we are born of God. We belong to Him—entirely! Consider these verses and the places where I've added emphasis that also talk about to whom we belong, who commissions us, who gives us our marching orders, and where our destinies lie:

- 1 John 4:7: "Beloved, let us love one another, for love is from God; and everyone who loves has been born of God and knows God."
- 1 John 5:1: "Whoever believes that Jesus is the Christ is born of God, and whoever loves the Father loves the child born of Him."
- John 13:16: "Truly, truly, I say to you, a slave is not greater than his master, nor is one who is sent greater than the one who sent him."
- John 14:28: "You heard that I said to you, 'I go away, and I will come to you.' If you loved Me, you would have rejoiced because I go to the Father, for the Father is greater than I."

SENT...

- John 14:31: "So that the world may know that I love the Father, I do exactly as the Father commanded Me."
- Matthew 28:20: "Teaching them to follow all that I commanded you."
- 1 John 3:23: "This is His commandment, that we believe in the name of His Son Jesus Christ, and love one another, just as He commanded us."

Therefore, whose mission are we on? Is it our mission, or is it Christ's? Jesus was on a mission which was birthed and initiated by the Father, designed by the Father, and directed by the Father as again verified by several of the above verses. If our mission is parallel to Christ's, whose mission are we on? Should it not be Christ's mission? We do not need to pray for His blessing over His mission because if we have been sent by Him, it is already blessed. Would He not have blessed it already? He would not send us on an errand or commission us to do something that He hadn't already blessed.

> **HE WOULD NOT SEND US ON AN ERRAND OR COMMISSION US TO DO SOMETHING THAT HE HADN'T ALREADY BLESSED.**

When I realized this, I stopped praying, "Jesus, bless me on my mission," but changed my prayer to the following: "Thank You that You have sent me on Your Mission, and as I am obedient to You in carrying this out, I thank You as I am receiving Your full support and blessing!" It changes things a whole lot! I have a renewed sense of faith when I pray this way. Faith is recognizing what God has done or is doing or is about to do! We switch from a beggar mentality, which is trying to plead with God to do something or inform Him of what He should be doing, to one of accepting by faith what He is doing and lining up our prayers, plans, and actions with those of His!

UNDER WHOSE CHARGE?

Without a doubt, I realized under whose charge Jesus was—that of the Father. I then asked myself, *Under whose charge am I to do the work of His kingdom?* Considering this, I then wondered, *What rights did Jesus have? What rights did He have to do what He did and say what He said?* Frankly, I was quite surprised at the number of times Jesus mentioned that He was sent of the Father to defend His actions, especially in relation to the Pharisees and temple rulers who represented the religious authority of that time.

After the affair of the woman caught in adultery was over, a discussion continued to brew and the Pharisees said to Jesus in John 8:13, "You are testifying about Yourself; Your testimony is not true." In other words, they claimed Jesus was on His own.

However, hear Jesus's reply:

"Even if I do testify on my own behalf, my testimony can be verified, because I know where I came from and where I am going. But you do not know where I come from or where I am going. You judge by appearances, but I do not judge anyone. And even if I should judge, my judgment is valid, because I am not alone, but it is I and the Father who sent me. Even in your law it is written that the testimony of two men can be verified. I testify on my behalf and so does the Father who sent me. —John 8:14-18

SENT...

Jesus claimed He was under commission—not alone. He clearly stated that His authority came in the way of Him who sent Him. The crowd would have gladly seized Him upon His stating who His authority was, but being under divine commission, John 8:20 says, "He spoke these words while teaching in the treasury in the temple area. But no one arrested him, because *his hour had not yet come.*"

It seems to me here that even the "times" were controlled by the Father as the One in supreme control of all things. Scripture then goes further with verse 25:

So they were saying to Him, "Who are You?" Jesus said to them, "What have I been saying to you from the beginning? I have many things to say and to judge regarding you, but, He who sent Me is true; and the things which I heard from Him, these I say to the world."

They did not realize that He had been speaking to them about the Father.

They were saying: "Who do you think you are?" Jesus did not back off but affirmed He was who He had said He was from the beginning. Then Jesus backed Himself up in having authority to say what He did with the answer: "He who sent Me." Jesus makes it plain that He is under the charge of the Father and that He only repeats things He'd heard from the Father. Of course, they did not understand this. But Jesus got His information from the One who sent Him—the Father. Jesus had heard the Father.

Where do we get our information? Whom do we hear? How much of what we do and say comes from what Christ is saying to and through us? When we are speaking the things which we have heard from Christ, can we not take courage to declare them without the fear of man, circumstances, or situations?

> **WHEN WE ARE SPEAKING THE THINGS WHICH WE HAVE HEARD FROM CHRIST, CAN WE NOT TAKE COURAGE TO DECLARE THEM WITHOUT THE FEAR OF MAN, CIRCUMSTANCES, OR SITUATIONS?**

I realize one can go to all kinds of extremes with this. It's hard to argue with someone who says: "God says so!" Yet we cannot throw the baby out with the bath water, either. There are safeguards in the written Word of God, spiritual authorities and family for our protection, along with fellow Christians and ministries that often bring the needed balance to those extreme things that violate the Word of God! Generally, those who take advantage by going to extremes do so with a haughty, prideful attitude and spirit. The fruit of these people's lives usually tell the tale:

"Beware of the false prophets, who come to you in sheep's clothing, but inwardly are ravenous wolves. You will know them by their fruits. Grapes are not gathered from thorn bushes nor figs from thistles, are they? So every good tree bears good fruit, but the bad tree bears bad fruit. A good tree cannot bear bad fruit, nor can a bad tree bear good fruit. Every tree that does not bear good fruit is cut down and thrown into the fire. So then, you will know them by their fruits.

"Not everyone who says to Me, 'Lord, Lord,' will enter the kingdom of heaven, but the one who does the will of

SENT...

My Father who is in heaven will enter. Many will say to Me on that day, 'Lord, Lord, did we not prophesy in Your name, and in Your name cast out demons, and in Your name perform many miracles?' And then I will declare to them, 'I never knew you; leave Me, you who practice lawlessness.'" —Matthew 7:15-23

This puts the fear of God into my heart. We can be on all kinds of missions, causes, and even do it in His name. But note that it is only doing the will of the Father that actually qualifies you. This is neither a matter of choice nor something casual—it is, indeed, very serious.

There will be plenty of those who will doubt, saying that God does not talk to us today. They will throw out all kinds of cautions that fall on the far end of the spectrum. Those people discourage any thought of God speaking, leading, or giving direction in our lives to do the work of the kingdom. Yet the Bible is full of examples where God spoke not only with the prophets, apostles, and ministers but also through people of all kinds, ages, and callings.

I heard someone state recently: "Isn't it strange that when we speak to God, we call this 'prayer,' but when we say God speaks to us, that puts us in the category of being a 'psychological' basket case?" We understand very well how important it is for God to speak to us. I say this simply because of the fact that Jesus is with us as a friend and companion. If He is our friend, then we should engage in two-way conversations with Him. Much more could be expounded on the subject and many great books have been written on the subject. Dr. Mark Virkler, a good friend of many

Marching Orders

years whom I learned a lot from, has a wealth of material on this subject in his Communion with God Ministries.[5]

I often wondered why Jesus prayed, and now I understand—He listened a whole lot to what the Father had to say to Him. I learn from this that my praying should consist of more listening to what Jesus is saying to me than what I am saying to Him.

This brings us back to John 8, where Jesus expounded in verses 28 and 29:

"I do nothing on My own, but I say these things as the Father instructed Me. And He who sent Me is with Me; He has not left Me alone, for I always do the things that are pleasing to Him."

Can we grasp this? He actually says that He could do nothing of His own initiative! Let me remind you here that this is Jesus speaking! Yes—nothing by His own initiative!

That conclusion brings me to my knees with conviction!

What have I done by my own initiative in the name of God? What have we all conjured up and planned with our genius, inspired minds, well-organized committees, well-balanced thinking, projected planning, and well-thought-out blueprints of our own initiative? Then we proceed to ask for God's blessing on it and call it a day.

Tell me, whose charge are we under, whose command? Whose directions do we follow?

If not a person's, then what circumstance propels us forward or holds us back? So often, I have seen Christians let circumstances determine the will and purpose of God. "It did not work out, so I guess it wasn't the will of God." "I do not have the resources,

---

[5] Communion with God Ministries, https://www.cwgministries.org/.

SENT...

time, or energy, so I don't think it is God." "It is too difficult," or "It has never been done before." Because of all these excuses, we abandon His calling. Do we actually think God is tied to our resources, time, energy, or difficult, limited situations? Do you think circumstances ever stopped God from preforming His will? I do not think so!

> **DO WE ACTUALLY THINK GOD IS TIED TO OUR RESOURCES, TIME, ENERGY, OR DIFFICULT, LIMITED SITUATIONS? DO YOU THINK CIRCUMSTANCES EVER STOPPED GOD FROM PREFORMING HIS WILL? I DO NOT THINK SO!**

On top of all of this, Jesus continued by saying that He always did the things that were pleasing to His Father. Again, I bow down in conviction and ask how many things I've done in the name of Christ that were actually what I liked or what pleased me, whether it be a committee, an adventure, some action, endeavor, or organization, or whatever the means may be, labeling it the work of God simply because I like it or it fits, though I've never taken the time to discover if any of it is pleasing to Him? Why not start off in the first place by asking Him, "What pleases You?" Perhaps even, "What do You want accomplished, and how, when, and where?" Under whose charge are you?

In saying this, I trust that you understand. I have worked with organizations, committees, churches, and boards. You name it, I've done it. Today, I am personally accountable to my organization: The Apostolic Church of Pentecost of Canada. I am also accountable as a missionary to the Estonian Christian Pentecostal

Church in Estonia, though I am also one of the founders. I am accountable to the board of the Village of Hope in Estonia as well as Canada, though I'm also a cofounder. I am personally accountable as a minister. I am not talking about a lone wolf attitude or some high-flying independent individual who claims no accountability to anyone but God, doing his own thing in the name of God. We all need to be accountable and work under godly structure and authority. We find this principle of submission and order in the life of Christ and His teachings in every way.

In this book, I am addressing us all: leaders, those who are led, committee members, board members, people in other positions, those without a position or title, pastors, and laity—from the least to the greatest. None is greater than Christ Himself, yet He made Himself least and a servant of all. I am calling upon all of us to be considered as "Sent" in the full context of Christ who said: "Peace be with you; as the Father has sent Me, I also send you" (John 20:21).

Let us return again to the many other verses where Jesus states this principle as a premise for His actions. We can go on and on, all the way to John 8:42: "Jesus said to them, 'If God were your Father, you would love Me, for I came forth and have come from God, for I have not even come on My own, but He sent Me.'"

So often, we say Christ chose to come to earth—no, that is not so. He was given. One of the most quoted Bible verses confirms this: "For God so loved the world, that He gave His only begotten Son, that whoever believes in Him shall not perish, but have eternal life" (John 3:16). In John 9:4, we see: "We must work the *works of Him who sent Me* as long as it is day; night is coming when no one can work." John 7:16 states: "So Jesus answered

SENT...

them and said, 'My teaching is *not Mine, but His who sent Me.*'"
And John 28:29 adds:

> Then Jesus cried out in the temple, teaching and saying, "You both know Me and know where I am from; and I have not come of Myself, but He who sent Me is true, whom you do not know. I know Him, because I am from Him, and He sent Me."

> **SO OFTEN, WE SAY CHRIST CHOSE TO COME TO EARTH—NO, THAT IS NOT SO. HE WAS GIVEN.**

He so angered the crowds by this that they wanted to take hold of Him, but because He was under "divine charge," they could not. Verse 30 says, "So they were seeking to seize Him; and no man laid his hand on Him, because *His hour had not yet come.*"

He walked in the Father's will and timing. If He was sent, then He was protected by the One who sent Him. This is another principle of the timing of God. If we are about His business and under His charge, then He has the perfect timing for it and protection over it. This does not mean the enemy will not oppose us, attack us, or try to interfere such as what we saw with the crowd around Jesus, but God had his timing, protection, and plan that was stronger than the opposition.

Then John 6:44 says: "No one can come to Me unless the Father who sent Me draws him; and I will raise him up on the last day." Again, the Father was doing the drawing. We do not "lead people to Jesus;" we obey Him to preach the gospel and proclaim the kingdom of God, but it is the work of the Father to draw them to Christ. Even Jesus did not draw the people to Himself. The Father sent, and the Father drew. How do we proclaim the kingdom as we evangelize? Preaching, witnessing, and proclaiming the gospel is not a slick sales job we pitch. It is a work of the Holy Spirit in action. The Spirit of God doing His work.

It is amazing just looking at these scriptures to see how active God really is! And ironically, we pray and think we are going to convince God to get moving or do something to reach the lost. We, endlessly, in what often seems to be great prayer meetings, spend time instructing and coaxing God for a so-called revival. He wants us to listen to what, where, and how He is doing it; then He will instruct us how to be an active part of what He is doing! Revival comes as a result of our obedience to a very active God who moves endlessly, in every realm of this earth and more!

I had a great missionary mentor, often referred to as "Bill Drost the Pentecost," teach me many things during travels and visits with him in Canada, Spain, and Europe that have stayed with me all my life. He would often say: "Find out what God is doing, and get in on it!"

As a young teenage boy, I would listen wide-eyed to the missionary tales he would tell in camp meetings and churches. Today, I understand why he had such great stories to tell. He was where the action was—he was wise enough to be a part of what God was doing and never bothered trying to coerce God into doing anything else.

At one youth conference in Chipman, New Brunswick in Eastern Canada, near where I grew up in the village of Gagetown, Bill Drost was speaking, and we were given a chance to place questions in a question box. The well-admired missionary would then, in an afternoon session, take time to answer these

SENT...

publicly. I put a question in the box about which I was very sincere: "Every time I hear a missionary speak, I have a desire to go to that country. How should I know which country to go to because I want to go to them all?" He drew out one question after another and commented on all sorts of youth issues and more. I eagerly waited for my question to turn up—and so it did.

I sat on the edge of my bench in the church and listened, breathlessly waiting with anticipation, to the answer as he read off the question. "That's a great question," Bill commented with enthusiasm, "I would not so much worry about *where* you should go. The important thing is that I see you have an open heart, and when the time is right, God will show you where you should be."

He was so right. Little did I realize what that all meant. Today, I have pastored for thirteen years and have also been a missionary for at least thirty-eight years. I've served on missionary councils, worked with missionaries, smuggled Bibles behind the Iron Curtain, and to this day, I am still a missionary in the land of my forefathers, in the country of Estonia. During that time as a young teenager, this was something that would have certainly been impossible to even dream about, due to Communism and the Iron Curtain. I followed exactly what Bill had advised that afternoon at the youth conference in Chipman, and God did the rest. As a matter of fact, though not a missionary for Spain, I was ordained into the ministry on the missionary field of Spain in the city of Madrid by our missions director Rev. Wynn Stairs, former Bible school director Rev. E. P. Wickens, two leaders of the Colombian Pentecostal movement Compo Bernal and Zuniga, and ironically, none other than the same missionary who answered my question that afternoon at the youth conference—Bill Drost himself!

This is how Jesus operated and now sends us to operate! In the same way, how do we operate, in whose way do we tend to do things, and in who's name do we blaze the trail of evangelization, church work, and gospel activities?

WHOSE IDEA WAS THIS ANYWAY?

This all causes me to realize how often we go on a mission, even if it is good, ask God to bless it, and ask Him to do something great with it. We are to be on God's mission and find out what He is doing and find our place in His mission—not His place in our mission! We so often create certain plans, both big and small, then inform God about these plans. On top of it all, we are brazen enough in our prayers to command God to start doing something about it. This is to our shame! Who gives us ideas anyway? Whose plans are we so busy with? Whose idea were they?

> **WE ARE TO BE ON GOD'S MISSION AND FIND OUT WHAT HE IS DOING AND FIND OUR PLACE IN HIS MISSION— NOT HIS PLACE IN OUR MISSION!**

Jesus says in John 5:19: "Jesus answered and said to them, 'Amen, amen, I say to you, a son *cannot do anything on his own*, but only what he sees his father doing; for what he does, his son will do also,'" and then in verse 30, Jesus says, "*I cannot do anything on my own;* I judge as I hear, and my judgment is just, because I do not seek my own will but the will of the *one who sent me.*"

I also like the way the KJV puts it: "*I can of mine own self do nothing:* as I hear, I judge: and my judgment is just; because I

SENT...

seek not mine own will, but the will of *the Father which hath sent me.*" Or set forth very explicitly in the MSG translation (vv. 30-33 and 36):

> *"I can't do a solitary thing on my own: I listen, then I decide. You can trust my decision because I'm not out to get my own way but only to carry out orders. If I were simply speaking on my own account, it would be an empty, self-serving witness. But an independent witness confirms me, the most reliable Witness of all. . . . for the works that the Father has given me to accomplish—the very works that I do—testify about Me, that the Father has sent me."*

I want to briefly pause here to make something very clear. I know today there are those who have taken this to the other extreme, and many will not do anything unless they have specifically heard from God. They often sit in the same place in their lives and walk with the Lord, being exactly where they were months before, a year ago, many years go, or worse, an entire lifetime. They are simply, as the old term I used to hear, "waiting on the Lord." It sounded spiritual enough, but the results were zero. They often waited for some magical moment, outstanding change of events, or some mystical sign from God that it was time to do whatever they thought it was God wanted them to do. These same people would often say, "the Lord willing." This scripture in context is not speaking about the plan of God in your life, but instead of a dependence upon, a recognition of, and an acknowledgement of God:

> *Yet you do not know what your life will be like tomorrow. For you are just a vapor that appears for a little while,*

and then vanishes away. Instead, you ought to say, "If the Lord wills, we will live and also do this or that." But as it is, you boast in your arrogance; all such boasting is evil. —James 4:14-16

It is here that God warns of an arrogant and boasting attitude, dependence on the self, and our tendency to neglect the frailty of life and thus shirk our dependence on God. It is not something we simply repeat as a phrase, but an attitude and lifestyle. Overall, what we say in this book is in the spirit of such an attitude, not just on certain occasions and instances of our comings and goings, events, and occurrences.

In Acts 10:38, it was recorded of Jesus:

"You know of Jesus of Nazareth, how God anointed Him with the Holy Spirit and with power, and how He went about doing good and healing all who were oppressed by the devil, for God was with Him."

We have ample scripture to support the fact that we are to preach the kingdom, do good, love one another, and be a light in a dark world. These are things we should be naturally doing as an outgrowth of our Christian beliefs and nature. We do not need specific instructions before we are allowed to carry out these things.

Let's just take "good" in light of the fact that Jesus went about doing it.

The Bible is filled with scriptures in reference to doing good. Let's look at the emphasized list.

- "Trust in the Lord and do good; Live in the land and cultivate faithfulness." (Psalm 37:3)

SENT...

- "Learn to do good; Seek justice, Rebuke the oppressor, Obtain justice for the orphan, Plead for the widow's case." (Isaiah 1:17)
- "Let's not become discouraged in doing good, for in due time we will reap, if we do not become weary." (Galatians 6:9)
- "But as for you, brothers and sisters, do not grow weary of doing good." (2 Thessalonians 3:13)
- "And do not neglect doing good and sharing, for with such sacrifices God is pleased." (Hebrews 13:16)
- "How much more valuable then is a person than a sheep! So then, it is lawful to do good on the Sabbath." (Matthew 12:12)
- "But I say to you who hear, love your enemies, do good to those who hate you." (Luke 6:27)
- "Do not be overcome by evil, but overcome evil with good." (Romans 12:21)

Here in Hebrews 13:21, we find that doing good is directly connected to His will: "Equip you in every *good* thing to *do* His will, working in us that which is pleasing in His sight, through Jesus Christ, to whom be the glory forever and ever. Amen." And in James 1:17, we are told everything good is that which comes from the Father: "Every *good thing* given and every perfect gift is from above, coming *down from the Father* of lights, with whom there is no variation or shifting shadow."

We have just brought your attention to doing good. There are dozens of other subjects such as love, patience, consideration, endurance, sharing, giving, and more. These are all things we do out of the character of being born of God as Christians. We do not wait for God to tell us to do these things, though it might be that we need reminders. But generally, we do these because of

Marching Orders

who we are and because the Spirit of God is within us: "But the fruit of the Spirit is love, joy, peace, patience, kindness, goodness, faithfulness, gentleness, self-control; against such things there is no law" (Galatians 5:22-23).

It is clear we need to live out who we are and do good in alignment with our character. We cannot just sit there and do nothing. That is like trying to live without breathing. But when we start to breathe, we are ready to move on to why we have the breath to breathe in the first place.

The best thing to do to find out the plan of God for your life is start moving! For instance, start doing good. I have a motto in my life: "Start with what you have, not with that which you don't have." When you start with what you have, you usually start to move. We all have something; move with it. If you sit there waiting and dreaming about all the things you do not have before you do something, then you will end up sitting there as a dreamer with no results. The Bible even says in James 4:17 (KJV), "Therefore to him that knoweth to do good, and doeth it not, to him it is sin."

So, the fact stands that we need to do what is at hand, what is commanded in the Word of God, His will, and His purpose in all the earth and in our lives. As we start with this and what is at hand, we are already moving and flowing with God. Only then will the *when* and *where* become clearer as we receive the instructions from the One Who has sent us for a specific task, fully in alignment for the purpose you were born to accomplish. You will accomplish whatever assignment is before you and whatever it is that He wants you to take on that will be fully backed by His commission, strength, guidance, protection, and supply.

SENT...

> **YOU WILL ACCOMPLISH WHATEVER ASSIGNMENT IS BEFORE YOU AND WHATEVER IT IS THAT HE WANTS YOU TO TAKE ON THAT WILL BE FULLY BACKED BY HIS COMMISSION, STRENGTH, GUIDANCE, PROTECTION, AND SUPPLY.**

Case in point: I remember well returning from an exhausting trip of smuggling my first Bibles behind the Iron Curtain. It was the beginning of August 1990 and my life-long friend Paul Prosser and I had taken a missions trip to Europe. I actually cannot say God had directly spoken to us to go, but we took the adventure because of the general interest we had in missions and desire to visit missionaries in Spain and churches in Holland, Germany, and Sweden.

Growing up, throughout all our childhood days, we were involved in church and developed an interest in missions. Paul's aunt, Elizabeth Steeves, was a missionary in India and on furlough to Paul's home, and her stories and adventures at our church piqued our interest. On the top of our list in visiting Europe was the land of my forefathers, Estonia, which had been occupied by the Soviet Union since the end of World War II. This would be the missionary trip we had talked and dreamed about. In Holland, we met senior Dutchman Peter Quist who had built a church housing a passionate congregation in Rotterdam—Filadelfia. I had met him earlier when he visited and spoke at our Bible school in Canada. The church in Rotterdam quite unexpectedly bought us a little Dutch two-cylinder DAF automobile, and we picked up a former Bible school friend, Greg Pine, who was studying in

Belgium, and the three of us set out for Spain to visit none other than Bill Drost and many of the workers and churches started under his ministry.

The days were filled with adventure, excitement, and ministry. It was like "missions alive." These sometimes routine days on the mission field with a missionary like Bill were a live introduction not only to missions but what God was preparing for each one of us, especially for myself. I would have never gotten to the next steps of God's work in my life had I not gone on these travels that, at times, seemed exciting though also became a predictable day-to-day norm of travel.

We drove back to Holland and there, through Rev. Quist, we were introduced to Brother Andrew, the author of the well-known book *God's Smuggler*. Upon hearing our desire to go to Estonia, the small-statured, intense Dutchman, who had smuggled thousands of Bibles behind the Iron Curtain, shouted with glee:

"Oh, I have these fifty big hard-covered Estonian Bibles in my warehouse and have not known what to do with them—if God has called you to go to Estonia, then please, help yourself, and take them with you!"

Not exactly knowing any better, we took them all, and to our delight, were on our way to Sweden and on to Helsinki, Finland, to catch a ship to Tallinn. We were filled with vision and purpose but scared out of our minds at the same time. The story is too lengthy, exciting, and intense to relay here, but it can be summarized with the following.

In short, Paul and I drove with our little DAF through Sweden to an Estonian family—the Laurs—who pastored the Estonian speaking congregation in Stockholm. They were such a blessing

SENT...

and help. Little did I realize the eldest son, Allan, would one day play such a great role in my own life. We moved from there to Helsinki. Against all odds, we got visas and Veikko Manninen, a highly celebrated Finnish pastor who hosted us, took us to the ship with our suitcases of Bibles and announced: "Let me take a picture of you both, so when you have been in Siberia for some years, we will all remember what you looked like, and we will be praying!"

What followed was a hair-raising, extraordinary smuggling operation of Bibles through the harbor of Tallinn, right under the noses and watchful eye of the Soviet customs officials on duty. Meeting youth aflame with hope and expectation, in spite of the impossible mission, these youth exclaimed: "We know how it is done!"

"How?" I asked.

The answer came immediately: "Simple! We pray, God does a miracle, and you bring the Bibles through!"

And so it happened. Scared out of our minds but not daring to show it, we tramped through customs with load after load of Bibles, until the agents got angry with us, shouting at us and telling us we could not just go running back and forth like that—either we needed to stay on shore or remain on the ship. But it happened: We got all the Bibles into the hands of those who were desperately waiting to receive them.

On our return back to Helsinki, I sat on the deck of the ship, tired and exhausted. I had met my relatives for the first time ever. My heart was sad to see how they lived in their own beloved land with no freedom—like a huge prison. This was the land I heard my parents talk so often about. On the other hand, I saw the eager youth so filled with hope and faith in God. I decided I would never return. It was just too much.

Then, all of a sudden, so unexpectedly, so swiftly and full of life, came the voice of God in my very innermost being. So you can understand, as I am sure so many have experienced it also, it was like a deep unexpected idea, impression, impulse, or gut feeling translated into words: *If you do not help these youth, who will? I want you to go back and help them.* I knew it was none other than the voice of God. I knew I had to come back—I had no choice. How, when, and where was not even in the equation, but I knew that was it, and not once ever did I doubt it, not even for a minute.

I knew I had received my marching orders.

I KNEW I HAD RECEIVED MY MARCHING ORDERS.

Did I immediately go back that same moment? No, but it was clear what I had to start preparing for. Had I not taken it into hand to "do good" with what I had, would the rest have followed? I can't answer that because I had done all I could, and when that was done, God did what He did, and the plan continued, as I believe He had designed. Through story after story of preparation, work, faith, and doing what was reasonable, the impossible became possible, followed by miracles. When we knew of nothing else and were often unaware of the danger and how to prepare, we repeatedly heard the voice of the Lord. After all, it was His mission, His orders, and His work for people who were in need.

The year following my marriage, my wife, Alta, and I did indeed return. The years that followed saw thousands of Bibles cross the

SENT...

Soviet border, as many as 6,700 in one single night and 28,100 during that same summer. Thousands of kilometers were driven, stretching over treacherous roads and impossible situations. If not for the continual ongoing promptings of the Holy Spirit and the instantaneous unexpected whisper of God's direction deep within our hearts, the solutions to these seemingly impossible situations would not have come. Yet, even at that, on the borders or deep in the USSR, far from any known help, I would at times feel overwhelmed, like God had stayed on the other side of the border, a million miles away, having left us to wander around in an unknown godless desert of some kind, totally abandoned. Yet it was with a grounded conviction that I overruled my feelings, knowing I was under divine commission, having been given marching orders, and that the One who "Sent..." me would back me up.

We learn about the relationship Jesus had with the Father across many scriptures and on what premises He worked as the One who sent Jesus to do these things. When we understand we are sent by Him, we can evaluate the things we are doing and why we are doing them—even to the fact which was mentioned just earlier in what He says in John 6:44: "No one can come to me unless *the Father who sent me draws him,* and I will raise him on the last day."

This makes me realize I am not the one, so called, winning souls or even bringing them to Jesus! I am just the worker working in the harvest of those whom the Father is bringing to Himself. I become the laborer and the proclaimer of His kingdom, allowing God to work through me. God is supreme in doing His work! I submit to Him. He commands us and sends us out into the harvest. I am the one who becomes the declarer of the good news of the gospel, proclaiming the kingdom of God. I dare not but hear, obey His commands, and walk in His ways, doing it and accomplishing it His way!

Let's get back to our subtitle: *Whose Idea Was This Anyway?* The answer to this question is obvious, and it should all be His idea in the first place!

Today, I realize why I work with those struggling with addiction in Estonia. As I said previously, it was never my desire, I was not very well-versed or educated in chemical addiction, nor had I personally experienced drugs and alcoholism. Yet, when I had given the work of the organized church over to others, I did it as an act of obedience to what the Lord had instructed. Because He previously told me, *You have not touched this nation as of yet until you reach those who are in utmost despair and darkness*, that is why there is a Village of Hope. That is why I then started to learn all I could about those in chemical addiction and how they could be helped.

If it had not been for my son Andrew and his obedience to God's plan to clue me in to what he knew, had lived, and was trained for, there would be no Village of Hope. Yes, I had to work hard to study and equip myself for the task at hand. Without Andrew's help, I could have never done it. It was part of God's overall plan, coming together with obedience and work on all sides. Without a doubt, I believe it was the will of God and the exclusive purpose of God for that phase of my life. What is success? In life, I believe I continue to learn one thing: it is making every effort to be obedient to Christ and do His will! That is success!

SENT...

> **WHAT IS SUCCESS? IN LIFE, I BELIEVE I CONTINUE TO LEARN ONE THING: IT IS MAKING EVERY EFFORT TO BE OBEDIENT TO CHRIST AND DO HIS WILL!**

As I work today with those in addiction, I see something much bigger developing than what I could foresee or understand at first. I have just seen the beginning of a bigger plan which God has for those whom He is calling out of this horrible pit of darkness. Out of this abyss of misery and destruction comes those who today are attending Bible school, preaching the gospel, starting new church plants, and doing the work of His kingdom. God has a super plan, much greater than what I can or even need to understand. But what I do understand is that I am only a part of it as one who has been sent and commissioned—and if so, there is only one way to do it all—His Way!

So again, I come back to the question with only one correct answer: "Whose Idea Was This Anyway?"—it was His!

WHAT CHOICE DO I HAVE?

If it is all His idea and initiative, then what choices do I have? Remember, John 20:21 says,
"It was the Father who sent me, and I am now sending you in the same way." Do we have a choice? Yes, I believe we do. This choice is fairly straight-forward and simple; it is to submit and obey... or do it our way. I find only one example of where Jesus openly struggled with this choice, which was at the garden of Gethsemane:

> *Then Jesus came with them to a place called Gethsemane, and told His disciples, "Sit here while I go over*

there and pray." And He took Peter and the two sons of Zebedee with Him, and began to be grieved and distressed. Then He said to them, "My soul is deeply grieved, to the point of death; remain here and keep watch with Me." —Matthew 26:36-38

This was pretty personal and intense. He made an attempt to share with His disciples the very pain of this decision, which was ripping His soul apart. He even looked for their support which failed Him:

And He went a little beyond them, and fell on His face and prayed, saying, "My Father, if it is possible, let this cup pass from Me; yet not as I will, but as You will." And He came to the disciples and found them sleeping, and He said to Peter, "So, you men could not keep watch with Me for one hour? Keep watching and praying, so that you do not come into temptation; the spirit is willing, but the flesh is weak." —Matthew 26:39-41

Jesus was left here alone with His very personal challenge. Others could not carry this for Him nor even did they make much effort. It burdened Him so heavily that finally He left the others and went ahead alone to pray. It was a personal moment to which He alone could answer. It was bearing on Him to the point the Bible says that He fell on His face and prayed. He fell on His face. He was gripped with the weight of it. The plea was an agonizing one, "If at all there was any other way then let it pass!" Then came the submission in the truest sense of the word: "Yet not as I will, but *as You will.*"

As if this was not enough, the moment almost repeated itself in Matthew 26:42: "He went away again a second time and prayed,

SENT...

saying, "My Father, if this cup cannot pass away unless I drink from it, *Your will be done.*" Once again, the decision and answer comes loud and clear: "*Your will be done.*" I cannot imagine how it felt in verse 43 when: "Again, He came and found them sleeping, for their eyes were heavy."

He was alone. When all was said and done, it was Him alone.

> **THERE COMES A TIME WHEN YOU STAND AT THE CROSSROADS OF DOING IT YOUR WAY OR HIS WAY.**

And so it is. There comes a time when you stand at the crossroads of doing it your way or His way. No one can make the decision for you—you know what you must do. This is where it is your choice. It is very personal and very real. The weight of such a decision falls directly on your very own shoulders. It is not an easy place to be, but only you can make that decision. It is a place where we often stand all alone. Just you and Jesus. No one else seems to understand, or even be there, like the disciples sleeping. It can seem a lonely place but it is where you need to be to come to grips with the decision before you. But remember Jesus is there, as was the Father!

When I was reading this, I noticed something I had never noticed before in Matthew 26:44-46:

> *And He left them again, and went away and prayed a third time, saying the same thing once more. Then He came to the disciples and said to them, "Are you still sleeping and resting? Behold, the hour is at hand and the Son of Man is being betrayed into the hands*

of sinners. Get up, let's go; behold, the one who is betraying Me is near!"

There was a third time. Yes, indeed there was a third time of Jesus "saying the same thing once more." It proves even further that this was not an easy decision. It was the circumstances, the feelings, the will, and the desire in a compelling struggle to submit and do what was right. Even for the third time—there alone again—yet it needed to be done. The disciples were still sleeping and resting, but He was not. This part was now over, and it was time to move on because the hour was at an end, and Scripture describes the rest. That did it. Case closed.

We have all at some time come to that place in our lives—usually not just once—perhaps several times. We can all remember them, some more dramatic than others, but they were there. They will always be there. It is never a one-time event in our lives, but as it occurs over and over, it soon becomes part of our lives, and it starts to shape the way we live and what is important to us. We soon discover that in like manner, the reward and fulfillment grow equally. We never regret making the choice because it is not our will but the Father's will.

This scripture in Matthew was the closest I could find to Jesus begging or pleading with the Father; it does not exist anywhere else. There wasn't even a hesitation to conclude His choice to submit. I do not find Him commanding the Father in any way, "Father, forget it; if You expect me to go through with this, I won't do it." I do not see anywhere where He is presenting a list of demands and expectations for the Father to perform, such as "If I do this and go through with it, then I expect You, Father, to take the pain away, give me a guarantee that I will come out on to top,

SENT...

or at least show me a sign. I expect compensation for My losses." I do not see Jesus crying out in despair or remorse, in self-pity or pleas such as, "Do You understand what this is costing Me? Who else has had to suffer like Me? Why Me? How long do You expect Me to put up with this?"

No, I see Him fully lined up with the will and purpose of the Father, confident to do what the Father has commanded Him to do, submitted to the will of the Father, and dependent on the resources and backing of the Father. It opened heaven's resources and provision. It opened God's will, bringing the best of possibilities into action on earth. It is something we all would long to live for and achieve! It is all there, but it is our choice to make.

Therefore, we are again pointed back to the awesome declaration Jesus now made when He said to us in John 20:21, "Peace be with you; as the Father has sent Me, I also send you."

In every form, shape, and fashion, the real truth of the matter is, just as Jesus was sent by the Father and submitted to being "Sent ..." so we are submitted to being "Sent...."

> **IN EVERY FORM, SHAPE, AND FASHION, THE REAL TRUTH OF THE MATTER IS, JUST AS JESUS WAS SENT BY THE FATHER AND SUBMITTED TO BEING "SENT..." SO WE ARE SUBMITTED TO BEING "SENT...."**

I had just turned nineteen and was entering my last year of high school in the village of Gagetown. I had a job at the F. W. Woolworth department store in the nearby Canadian military town of Oromocto. I liked my job, being in charge of the menswear department as well as walking the floor catching shoplifters. There was never a dull moment.

I had our church family camp coming up, and it was the spiritual highlight of my year—attending the services, listening to missionaries, eating at the big dining hall, meeting other youth from other churches from all over the province, the early morning and after meeting prayer meetings. It had been part of my spiritual growth and experience since I first went there as a child of nine years old, and I experienced the baptism of the Holy Spirit and was water baptized in the adjoining lake at Harvey Camp.

I asked my oversight at Woolworth if I could go to the camp. He assured me I could go. I was happy to be given the opportunity. Those ten days, including the weekend, were everything I had anticipated and more. When I arrived back at the store to resume my duties, Mr. Moore, the manager, met me at the information desk, and I was politely fired. I could not believe him. Do you know what he said?

"You just don't walk off your job and then expect to return. You are done."

I explained to him I had asked permission. But it was to no avail. I walked out the door and felt totally dejected. I asked myself, *Was it really worth it?* I sat in my car and prayed. I cannot remember the prayer, but in the middle of it, I came up with a thought, totally out of the blue. I knew of a poultry farm about fifty kilometers from my home in Gagetown. The owner would occasionally come to our small church to speak. His name was Harry Law of Law's Poultry Farm and Hatchery. I called him up that afternoon and learned that the farm was enlarging their facilities and building a new chicken barn. I was hired on immediately

SENT...

and went to work the next morning. The work was hard, but I enjoyed my weeks during the rest of the summer working beside big carpenter Clyde Venio.

Harry Law was very demanding, but I was willing to learn. I had seen him for some time at our church in Gagetown, and then one day, he pulled me aside and said how disappointed he was in the established church. He said his plan was to finance his own ministry and was considering how much money he would make an hour if he no longer attended his church, freed himself from tithing, and just stayed home to serve God there. I did not agree with his thinking and felt disappointed in his conclusions.

However, at the end of the summer, Harry made a proposition to me which made me listen with exhilarated enthusiasm. He would set me up in the poultry business with a job to buy chickens for a certain number of years from his hatchery. I shared the plan with my dad, and he was ecstatic about the opportunity, especially since we had the lands on our farm, and this was my last year at school. I felt I was on top of the world. It was the perfect opportunity and something I would love doing. I loved the farm by the river in Gagetown where I had grown up, and it would be a dream to live there and embark on such an adventure. I lived the dream over and over again in my mind. It was so perfect!

Then as I was pondering this in my mind for the hundredth time, another recollection suddenly came as if from nowhere. I remembered a day out in the barn as a young boy of thirteen. After feeding the pigs and chickens, gathering the eggs, and milking the cows, I would take the milking stool and shove it next to the pile of hay and kneel there in prayer. All of a sudden on that late summer afternoon, quite unexpectedly, it seemed like God Himself entered the barn. I did not see any visible signs and heard no audible voice, but it was there deep in my heart—a profound impression which I understood to be the voice of God: *I want you to serve me the rest of your life, and I want you to preach the gospel!* That was it. The words filled my very being. I jumped up with ecstatic joy, and with emotions bursting like an explosion, ran out the barn door and commenced to running around the barn, shouting with joy!

My first thought was, *I will become a "boy preacher!"* Though only going into the seventh grade, I would have delightfully quit school and begun to preach immediately! I shared my enthusiasm with my mom, thinking she would be delighted, and she was. Naturally, the whole idea of quitting school was out of the question. My dad, not a believer, found out some time later that I wanted to become a preacher and was totally appalled at the very idea that his son would even consider becoming a minister.

"At least become a ditch-digger," he resounded angrily one day when the subject came up. "That way you at least will earn an honest living. Sipping tea with the ladies during the week and delivering a little speech on Sunday are no way for a man to live!"

It would be years later during my Bible school training that he would even begin to acknowledge the validity of the call on my life. There did come the day that he was proud of what I had accomplished, although it was a long time coming, and he never really understood the depth of my experience and call.

I remember how I hardly knew where to begin, so in the same barn, I would lay my open Bible out on the feed box, use it as a pulpit, face the row of cows feeding in their stalls, and preach to the cows! I do not know if they produced better quality milk or

SENT...

what, if anything, went through their minds, but I know what was happening in this young boy's heart, mind, and soul. This was now a part of my life. When I look back on this, I think it was a pretty good place to start for anyone! I continued to preach wherever anyone would let me—in front of the town post office, on the street, out in the woods to the trees, at the main gates of the Oromocto, Camp Gagetown military training base (until the military police sent me away), and eventually in our church in Gagetown, where I would have to stand beside the pulpit because I could not see over it. To this very day, I have never stopped.

> **I WAS AT A CROSSROADS, AND IT WAS A TEMPTATION FAR GREATER THAN I HAD BARGAINED FOR.**

But now I was at a crossroads. There I stood, nineteen years old, and the choice was not easy. Especially considering my dad was totally relieved and jubilant since it would at least not be the ministry. It was a temptation far greater than I had bargained for. I then though of what Harry had said about building up a support base with his hatchery to do ministry. It seemed like such a good idea; I could do exactly that.

Out in the barn, I would pray in earnest, selling God on the idea of this excellent plan that had unfolded and how I had devised a perfect plan of financing my own ministry with the chickens I raised and income from poultry farming. For hours, I would pray presenting the whole idea with enthusiasm before God. I could just envision God all enthused and excited every bit as much as I was about the whole adventure. Then it happened, in one split second of silence—I heard the voice of God again: *My son, it will be either chickens or Me, not both. Either the chickens or Me.*

That was it. Nothing more. It was as plain as that. All of a sudden it became so clear to me. I saw Harry's plans go so wrong, preoccupied with thinking he could garner the support for his own ministry that eventually he did not even go to church, let alone participate in any ministry, because he had calculated how much he would save by not doing so. I made my decision to devote everything to Jesus. I never again looked back. My poor dad never understood and considered me to be a very foolish son for letting such a grand opportunity pass me by. I also did not understand the scope of what was ahead, but that was not important in that moment. The important thing was that I submit, and to submit meant to say, by Jesus's very own example in Matthew 26:39, "Yet not as I will, but *as You will*." To let His will be done—His way.

In the midst of it all, though my dad was so against my entering the ministry, he did not realize how much God was using him to prepare my destiny to eventually minister in Estonia. You see, since we were refugees and immigrants to Canada, it was a strong tradition for us to preserve our native language—the Estonian language. Without an exception, our language at home would be Estonian. That was the law, according to my father's thinking. There would be no exceptions. As children, when we strayed off and began to speak in English, our dad would come unexpectantly upon us, let out an oath, and command in the Estonian language: "Off to the woodshed! Right now! You get an armload of wood for the house!"

We well knew what that meant—rain or shine, snow or cold—on with the boots, coat, and gloves, and out to the woodshed.

SENT...

There, we would complain and mutter under our breath, "Where under God's heaven are we ever going to need this language?" There was only one family of Estonians who eventually continued to live in our village of Gagetown. "People hardly know where Estonia is," we would grumble, "let alone, use this language!" We would continue to complain while gathering up the armload of wood and say, "The poor old man still lives in some fairytale land across the ocean and has probably forgotten entirely that he lives in Canada!" But it changed nothing. My dad did not budge an inch.

Years later, when Estonia had regained its independence in 1991, my colleagues and I became actively involved in establishing the Estonian Christian Pentecostal Church. We were holding services in the former Communist cultural center called the Sakala, or as some had named it, Vaino Cathedral, after the Estonian Communist party secretary Karl Vaino.[6] My dad came to the Sunday service where several hundred Estonians were present. I thought I would introduce him; I was proud of the fact that he had come to the service at all: "I want to introduce to you someone special this morning—the man who sent me off to the woodshed to get wood in the Estonian language." They knew the story well; they had often heard me tell it. I continued, "Today I stand here and speak Estonian because of this man, my father!"

The crowd erupted into a thundering applause and standing ovation. My dad stood, overcome by total surprise with a completely startled look but at the same time, beaming all over and hands spread open. To me, the moment was priceless. I do not know what all happened in my dad's mind and heart that

---

6 "Karl Vaino," *Wikipedia*, https://en.wikipedia.org/wiki/KarlVaino.

moment—maybe memories, thoughts, opinions, or whatever else—but afterward, he told me with a chuckle and a pleasing smile on his face, while jabbing me on my shoulder, "Looks like I'm even more popular than you are!" I could tell he was rightfully proud, and I was happy for him.

We do not always know how it all ends, but God does. We need but only trust Him. He knows what He is doing. In that trust, we gain the strength to submit and make the right decisions. They don't always produce the answers right off, but they will come eventually. As difficult as it may have been, leading up to this point, what choice did I really have? I had but one: to obey my marching orders. It was His mission for my life, not mine. Yet at the same time, I knew it was the right one. Not always easy, yet the best. I was under His charge. It was His idea in the first place. I have never regretted it.

Not for a moment do I want a single word of this book that details my own life experiences to leave you with the impression that I have "arrived." I have discovered over and over again that despite being excited, convinced, and convicted about the truths I am presenting to you, I am still on a journey to stay humble, obedient, and in love with Jesus! We have a long way to go, and I hope you think about these things and join me in this journey, reevaluate the things we do, and while doing them, ask the question, "Who or what am I submitted to?" followed by the subtitle for this section, "What Choice Do I Have?"

Yes, indeed, I do have a choice. But then on the other hand . . . do I? I have a choice to decide whose way I go. Can I and will I trust Him with His marching orders? It is my choice.

SENT...

Due to the COVID-19 crisis, the year changed like the world had never experienced before. People have asked all kinds of questions:
- Is this the end times?
- What will we do now?
- Is this of God?
- Is this an onslaught of the demonic forces of hell?

To tell you the truth, I do whatever is reasonable in the responsibility I have to myself and others, continuing to submit to His will, to His purpose, and rely upon His direction to the best of my understanding of His guidance and Word. After all, He is still in control. There are no surprises for Him. He knows the beginning and the end. He knows where you and I fit in the middle of it all. I choose to trust Him and carry on.

> **GOD KNOWS THE BEGINNING AND THE END. HE KNOWS WHERE YOU AND I FIT IN THE MIDDLE OF IT ALL. I CHOOSE TO TRUST HIM AND CARRY ON.**

God gave me this theme in scripture for 2021, right in the midst of the pandemic, which I have kept close to my heart and have focused on in my thoughts even to this day—during the war in Ukraine happening directly on the border of Russia, which has so very keenly and directly affected us here in Estonia. As I sit here and write, I hear the roar of the NATO fighter jets, just ten kilometers (six miles) from here, going out on patrol and exercises. And so on it goes. What will happen in the days to come?

Marching Orders

It has all settled in my mind and heart in light of what the psalmist David penned in Psalm 24:1, "The earth is the Lord's, and the fullness of it, the world and they who dwell in it." It all still belongs to Him, no matter what. Circumstance do not change what God owns. I choose to believe this and keep marching on in the commission and orders I am given. I think it would be good to repeatedly pray the way Jesus taught us in Matthew 6:8:

"Do not be like them, for your Father knows what you need before you ask Him. Pray, therefore, like this: 'Our Father Who is in heaven, hallowed (kept holy) be Your name.

Your kingdom come, Your will be done on earth as it is in heaven.'"

Why, then, should I not submit myself to Him, preoccupy myself with His will and commands, and trust Him, the very One who gave me my marching orders in the first place? Matthew 10:7 says, "As you go, make this proclamation: 'The kingdom of heaven is at hand.'" And finally, Jesus says in Matthew 24:14, "And this gospel of the kingdom will be preached throughout the world as a witness to all nations, and then the end will come." Let's march on!

CHAPTER 4

TO WHAT OR TO WHOM ARE YOU SUBMITTING YOUR LIFE?

SUBMITTED ONE WAY OR ANOTHER

No matter how you look at it—something, someone, or maybe even you, is now ruling or will eventually rule your life one way or another. If it is not you or someone else, then it is some set of circumstances that will make your decisions and control your life. I can now look back to the decision I had to make as a youth and see why it was so necessary to understand what God was saying when He said, "Either the chickens or Me."

SENT...

Jesus taught this principle with one excerpt from the Sermon on the Mount: "No one can serve two masters; for either he will hate the one and love the other, or he will be devoted to one and despise the other. You cannot serve God and wealth" (Matthew 6:24). In every sense of the word masters, we are submitted to something or someone one way or another. As we emphasized in the previous chapter—the choice is ours.

How well are you doing?

> **OFTEN, PEOPLE THINK THEY ARE JUST NOT GOING TO DECIDE ANYTHING AT ALL AND INSTEAD CHOOSE TO REVERT TO SOME KIND OF PASSIVE MODE. IN REALITY, THEY HAVE ALREADY MADE A DECISION TO LET CIRCUMSTANCES DETERMINE THE OUTCOME.**

So often, people think they are just not going to decide anything at all and instead choose to revert to some kind of passive mode. In reality they have already made a decision to let circumstances determine the outcome. They may state: "Oh, it did not work out, so it must not have been the will of God." But was it?

Do circumstances then decide for us what the will of God is? If we do not take a stand or decision about what is right and in accordance to the will of God, then circumstances will decide for you, and you will be submitted to what it determines. They will then become your master because you have already submitted to them.

If I had let circumstance lead my life, it would have been much different and the will of God would have never been accomplished. I would have never scaled the impossibilities, done the unthinkable, or savored the sweetness of the satisfaction that pulses through my very being today. I have lived the life of fulfillment, living out the will and purpose of Christ, as He designed for me. Circumstance would have never allowed this. I needed to see beyond its grip, defy its piercing talons, and in faith, grasp the purposes of God for my life. None of the things I have told you would have happened. There would have been no Bibles cross the border, no churches planted or built, no Village of Hope for addicts, few (and maybe no) souls saved—because my circumstances would not have allowed room for any of these things.

So, since God had this plan for my life, from whom or from where could I have learned the most to practically apply to my life? Did Jesus just wander through His time on earth, a victim of circumstances and events, or did He live His life to satisfy and suit the desires and opinions of others... or even His own? I think we know the answer to this.

Therefore, would it not be reasonable to turn our attention to the example of Christ? After all, could and should we not look to Him for the pattern? Jesus did not speak much about theological issues, though He did He touch upon them. He usually taught to impart practical, day-to-day life application. But what Jesus did was teach a great deal on how man should live, the value and purpose of life, how we ought to treat one another, and the principles pertaining to life and how it should be lived.

As such, would Jesus Himself not have been born with a designed, destined purpose? It would be irrational to think otherwise!

Even during one of the most crucial moments of His life, Jesus stated with deep conviction:

SENT...

"Now My soul is troubled and deeply distressed; what shall I say? "Father, save Me from this hour [of trial and agony]"? But it is for this [very] purpose that I have come to this hour [this time and place]. —John 12:27 (AMP)

Shortly following this moment, He again pointed this out in detail to Pilate in John 18:37 (AMP):

So Pilate said to Him, "Then You are a King?" Jesus answered, "You say [correctly] that I am a King. This is why I was born, and for this I have come into the world, to testify to the truth. Everyone who is of the truth [who is a friend of the truth and belongs to the truth] hears and listens carefully to My voice."

It is very clear here that Jesus had a unique purpose in life. His arrest did not happen by chance, and He did not accidentally fail to escape those who wanted to kill Him.

> **IT IS VERY CLEAR HERE THAT JESUS HAD A UNIQUE PURPOSE IN LIFE. HIS ARREST DID NOT HAPPEN BY CHANCE, AND HE DID NOT ACCIDENTALLY FAIL TO ESCAPE THOSE WHO WANTED TO KILL HIM.**

Now, if Jesus had a purpose, which has already been proven throughout this book, you also have a life purpose. We can now weave the two together in an event in a powerful statement He made in the context of John 20. It brings us to the truth about our purpose for existing that no one can overlook or discount. It directs us on how we ought to live our lives in order to reach our fullest potential and accomplish the purpose He has given us from birth.

That is why I believe, that even before I was born, in the middle of the raging Baltic storm in the hull of old sailing vessel, people sobbing for fear, my mom not being able to stand on her feet, she dropped to her knees and prayed the prayer, "Lord, we need to get to Sweden . . . I will promise You if we get to Sweden, I will go to church every Sunday!" However this prayer may be evaluated, it was in the truest sense a desperate petition, but in the middle of that prayer was something of a plea that lined up with the very purposes of God for my life and what I am privileged to live out today in the purpose and will of God.

Let's look at it again. Jesus said in John 20:21 (NKJV): "So Jesus said to them again, 'Peace to you! As the Father has sent Me, I also send you.'"

Again, I draw your attention repeatedly to this for many reasons. First, it is very obvious that Jesus here said that He had been sent of the Father. This is very significant, even more than what you might realize. This is stated here very explicitly. We will study this further. But before we do, let us keep in mind that whatever we learn of His commission in being sent cannot be directly isolated to Himself as an individual because we are directly linked to this commission.

Remember, we are connected directly to this assignment by the fact that Jesus, being sent of the Father, went on to expound, "As the Father has sent me, I also send you." Let us not forget that not only did He simply state that he was sending us, but he began His statement with the small two-letter word, "as." Again,

SENT...

no matter how many translations we have used, it cannot be read any other way.

> **LET US NOT FORGET THAT NOT ONLY DOES HE SIMPLY STATE THAT HE IS SENDING US, BUT HE BEGINS HIS STATEMENT WITH THE SMALL TWO-LETTER WORD, "AS."**

Let's once again review a couple of these, as they are worth looking at. John 20:21 (NIV) says, "Again Jesus said, 'Peace be with you! As the Father has sent me, I am sending you.'" And again, in the NASB version, this verse reads, "So Jesus said to them again, 'Peace be with you; as the Father has sent Me, I also send you.'"

In light of the fact that we have now looked at the spiritual principles behind this verse, we may understand the depth of what is being said more clearly. Some of the translations bring out our connection to this commission even more distinctively as you can see from my emphases. For example, this verse in the World English version says, "Jesus therefore said to them again, 'Peace be to you. As the Father has sent me: *even so I send you*.'" The YLT version states, "Jesus, therefore, said to them again, 'Peace to you; *according as the Father hath sent me, I also send you*.'" The PHILLIPS version says it like this: "Yes, peace be with you! *Just as the Father sent me, so I am now going to send you.*" Finally, we have the ERV version: "Peace be with you. *It was the Father who sent me, and I am now sending you in the same way.*"

In other words, in the "same way" or in "like manner" that the Father had sent Jesus, now Jesus is sending us! Hang on to that for a second! The realization of that alone is mind boggling. To say the least, it encircles an unbelievable wide scope.

OUR JESUS CONNECTION

I have already introduced the subject, but moving forward, I would like to reinforce it by bringing it back into focus. That is, if we are sent by Jesus in the same manner as the Father sent Jesus, what better way for us to understand this commission than to study the life of Christ and learn how Jesus Himself related to His "being sent" of the Father. This would clarify our understanding of how we are sent and give us a perfect understanding of how we ought to relate to "being sent" by Jesus.

> **OF COURSE, THERE IS A LIVING CONNECTION BETWEEN JESUS AND THE FATHER. LIKEWISE, THERE IS A LIVING CONNECTION BETWEEN US AND JESUS.**

Of course, there is a living connection between Jesus and the Father. Likewise, there is a living connection between us and Jesus. John 6:57 reminds us, *"Just as the living Father sent Me, and I live because of the Father, the one who eats Me, he also will live because of Me."* Reading further, Jesus continues:

> *"After a little while, the world no longer is going to see Me, but you are going to see Me; because I live, you also will live. On that day you will know that I am in My Father, and you are in Me, and I in you."* —John 14:19-20

Our lives are totally connected to Christ. Look at John 6:57, "I live because of the Father, the one who eats Me, he also will live

SENT...

because of Me." We are so intertwined with Christ, so connected with the God of this universe! John 17:21 adds, "That *they* may all be one; even *as* You, *Father, are* in *Me and I in You*, that *they* also may be *in Us*, so that the world may believe that *You sent Me.*"

It's no wonder that after grasping this truth, Paul exclaimed in Galatians 2:20:

> *"I have been crucified with Christ; and it is no longer I who live, but Christ lives in me; and the life which I now live in the flesh I live by faith in the Son of God, who loved me and gave Himself up for me.*

Notice, again, the words that I've emphasized. Let's look at this in the context of the same chapter this book is centered around (John 20:21): "So Jesus said to them again, 'Peace be with you; as the Father has sent Me, I also send you.'"

Here, just a few verses before this in the continued story of His resurrection, Jesus said the most amazing thing to a clinging Mary, to indicate this connection in John 20:17:

> *Jesus said to her, "Stop clinging to Me, for I have not yet ascended to the Father; but go to My brothers and say to them, 'I am ascending to My Father and your Father, and My God and your God.'"*

Do you get it? What a connection! First of all—"My brethren," then, "My Father and your Father, and My God and your God." Note—"your Father" and "your God". Where does that put us in our union?

Many, still today, are like Mary, clinging to Christ. They say, "I'm holding on to Jesus!" as if having achieved some merit of self-effort, when the truth of the matter is much deeper than just hanging on to Him. We have been united, connected, and bonded with Christ by His work on the cross through His death, burial, and resurrection! We are brothers in Christ, born of the Father united with God Himself!

This is what the whole chapter of Romans 6 is all about. Here is one verse:

> *Therefore we have been buried with Him through baptism into death, so that, just as Christ was raised from the dead through the glory of the Father, so we too might walk in newness of life." —Romans 6:4*

> **THIS NEW LIFE IS NOW HIS LIFE IN US AND OURS IN HIM. IT IS MORE THAN JUST TURNING OVER A LEAF FOR A NEW START.**

This new life is now His life in us and ours in Him. It is more than just turning over a leaf for a new start. We are born all over again in spirit into a brand-new spiritual relationship. John 3 tells it in story form when Nicodemus made a visit to Jesus. In this same Gospel, it alone is filled with remarkable examples and statements of Christ Himself which gives us unbelievable insight into this vital subject. Again, I must say, the entire New Testament is full of examples of the life of Christ in respect to His real-life connection to the Father. This does not only give us the information we are looking for, but also challenges us to the core of our own being when we discover in Scripture the depth of our Jesus connection!

BY WHOSE ACTION?

How this relates to us is discussed in the first chapter of this book under the heading "By Whose Choice and Initiative?" Coming

SENT...

back to how Christ was sent, we see the element of God's initiative in action in the life of Jesus.

To begin with, in relation to Christ, whose initiative was it for Jesus to be born into this world? I misunderstood this for a long time, thinking it was the initiative of Christ Himself, coming and taking it upon Himself to save a lost humanity. Let's look at what the Bible says in Galatians 4:4: "But when the fullness of the time came, *God sent His Son*, born of a woman, born under the Law."

Further:

> *By this the love of God was manifested in us, that God has sent His only begotten Son into the world so that we might live through Him. . . . In this is love, not that we loved God, but that He loved us and sent His Son to be the propitiation for our sins. . . . We have seen and testify that the Father has sent the Son to be the Savior of the world.* —1 John 4:9, 10, and 14

We arrive at the most popular scripture, so often quoted, which again bears the truth of God's action of love to save mankind by sending His Son in John 3:16:

> *For God so loved the world, that He gave His only begotten Son, that whoever believes in Him shall not perish, but have eternal life. For God did not send the Son into the world to judge the world, but that the world might be saved through Him.*

JESUS WAS LINKED TO THE FATHER IN ALL OF HIS ACTIONS.

To What or to Whom Are You Submitting Your Life?

In John 5, we have Jesus healing the man who had been lying at the pool of Bethesda with a sickness that caused him to be lame for thirty-eight years. Jesus healed him. The Jews had no issue with that. But they did have an issue with the fact that Jesus did this on the Sabbath. That is, Jesus told him to take up his pallet and carry it on the Sabbath, which the Jews did not permit. When the Jews approached Jesus for doing these things on the Sabbath, Jesus immediately turned their attention to the fact that He was linked to the Father in His action:

The man went back and told the Jews that it was Jesus who had made him well. That is why the Jews were out to get Jesus—because he did this kind of thing on the Sabbath. But Jesus defended himself. "My Father is working straight through, even on the Sabbath. So am I." That really set them off. The Jews were now not only out to expose him; they were out to kill him. Not only was he breaking the Sabbath, but he was calling God his own Father, putting himself on a level with God.
—John 5:16-18 (MSG)

As stated, this really ticked them off, but Jesus continued His defense with:

"I'm telling you this straight. The Son can't independently do a thing, only what he sees the Father doing. What the Father does, the Son does. The Father loves the Son and includes him in everything he is doing.
—John 5:19-20 (MSG)

Jesus then went on further to clarify:

"For the Father loves the Son, and shows Him all things that He Himself is doing; and the Father will show Him

SENT...

> *greater works than these, so that you will be amazed. For just as the Father raises the dead and gives them life, so the Son also gives life to whom He wishes. For not even the Father judges anyone, but He has given all judgment to the Son, so that all will honor the Son just as they honor the Father. The one who does not honor the Son does not honor the Father who sent Him. Truly, truly, I say to you, the one who hears My word, and believes Him who sent Me, has eternal life, and does not come into judgment, but has passed out of death into life. —John 5:20-24*

Jesus's unbelievable exposition and discussion did not stop even at this point, but persisted with zeal. He continued throughout the chapter:

> *"I can do nothing on My own. As I hear, I judge; and My judgment is righteous, because I do not seek My own will but the will of Him who sent Me.... But the testimony I have is greater than the testimony of John; for the works which the Father has given Me to accomplish—the very works that I do—testify about Me, that the Father has sent Me. And the Father who sent Me, He has testified about Me. You have neither heard His voice at any time nor seen His form. Also you do not have His word remaining in you, because you do not believe Him whom He sent." —John 5:30, 36-38*

It is way beyond any doubt whose action of healing Jesus represented and performed on Sabbath at the pool of Bethesda that day. Jesus did not back off but concluded:

To What or to Whom Are You Submitting Your Life?

> *"But I know you, that you do not have the love of God in yourselves. I have come in My Father's name, and you do not receive Me; if another comes in his own name, you will receive him. How can you believe, when you accept glory from one another and you do not seek the glory that is from the one and only God? —John 5:42-44*

Jesus continued in John 7:3-10 while walking in Galilee at the Feast of the Booths. Here, Jesus was careful about where He went and to whom He showed Himself, even to the point of hiding, because it wasn't yet His appointed time:

> *So His brothers said to Him, "Move on from here and go into Judea, so that Your disciples also may see Your works which You are doing. For no one does anything in secret when he himself is striving to be known publicly. If You are doing these things, show Yourself to the world." For not even His brothers believed in Him. So Jesus said to them, "My time is not yet here, but your time is always ready. The world cannot hate you, but it hates Me because I testify about it, that its deeds are evil. Go up to the feast yourselves; I am not going up to this feast because My time has not yet fully arrived." Now having said these things to them, He stayed in Galilee. But when His brothers had gone up to the feast, then He Himself also went up, not publicly, but as though in secret.*

When time was right, he went ahead to teach publicly in the temple, boldly stating:

> *"My teaching is not My own, but His who sent Me. If anyone is willing to do His will, he will know of the teaching, whether it is of God or whether I speak from*

SENT...

> *Myself. The one who speaks from himself seeks his own glory; but He who is seeking the glory of the One who sent Him, He is true, and there is no unrighteousness in Him.* —John 7:16-18

And then with great openness and boldness, He cried out in the temple:

> "You both know Me and know where I am from; and I have not come of Myself, but He who sent Me is true, whom you do not know. I know Him, because I am from Him, and He sent Me. . . ." Therefore Jesus said, "For a little while longer I am with you, then I go to Him who sent Me. —John 7:28-29 and 33

It is beyond any reasonable doubt, over and over again, that Jesus implied with great clarity and conviction by whose direction He was working in John 8:42: "If God were your Father, you would love Me, for I came forth from God and am here; for I have not even come on My own, but He sent Me." Then, John 11:42, Jesus stated, "I knew that You always hear Me; but because of the people standing around I said it, so that they may believe that *You sent Me*." And in John 14:10-11, He said:

> "Do you not believe that I am in the Father, and the Father is in Me? The words that I say to you I do not speak on My own, but the Father, as He remains in Me, does His works. Believe Me that I am in the Father and the Father is in Me; otherwise believe because of the works themselves."

Can we get a hold of this? Jesus was saying very clearly, "I am in the Father," and "the Father is in Me," and even repeated this. A few verses later, Jesus then astonishingly declared in John 14:20,

"On that day you will know that *I am in My Father*, and *you are in Me*, and *I in you*."

What an astounding piece of information! It is more than information—it is the whole of the experience of being united with Christ! What is so incredible about this statement is that it reveals to us that our connection to Christ places us together with the Father, the God of the universe! It puts us right in the middle of our union with God! If we even began to think on this, it is more than the mind could absorb! It places us where we really are in this whole picture of being connected to Jesus!

The whole idea is so far reaching that it brings us into the very being of God and His plans and purposes for us personally and individually:

> *For those whom He foreknew, He also predestined to become conformed to the image of His Son, so that He would be the firstborn among many brethren; and these whom He predestined, He also called; and these whom He called, He also justified; and these whom He justified, He also glorified.* —Romans 8:29-31

This should leave no doubt in our minds by whose initiative the destiny of our lives are designed. We are so integrated into the person of Christ and therefore connected to God and His purposes—is it hard to believe otherwise? Could we understand it any other way than to know our destiny is sealed by His action?

MINDSET OF PURPOSE

Jesus not only acknowledged, which He so often did, that He was sent with the Father's words, but He also embodied a marked mindset of purpose affixed to the Father His entire life. He would

SENT...

not allow Himself to waver from His purpose which the Father had set for Him.

He illustrated this during the very trying moments of His life surrounding His arrest in John 18:11: "So Jesus said to Peter, 'Put the sword into the sheath; the cup which the *Father has given Me*, am I not to drink it?" His mind was made up. There would be no change in His decision to follow through with what the Father had designed as His destiny. This did not start with this occasion but was established with Christ from the very beginning, even as a child when He told His parents in Luke 2:49 (KJV), "How is it that ye sought Me? Wist ye not that I must be about *My Father's business*?"

> **IT WAS THE MINDSET OF BEING ABOUT MY FATHER'S BUSINESS THAT KEPT ME AWAY FROM ALL THE VARIOUS TEMPTATIONS WHICH WOULD HAVE LED ME OFF COURSE.**

Now, looking back on my own life, it is obvious that this is what I experienced and what stayed with me the rest of my life—the experience I had out in the cow barn at thirteen years of age when I sensed what seemed like the very presence of God entering the barn and speaking to my heart that I was to preach the gospel for the rest of my life. No other opportunity availed itself but to start where I was. Putting the Bible on the feed box, I preached to the cows! There was a sense in my heart that I, too, had to "be about My Father's business." It was this mindset of purpose that kept me away from all the various temptations which would have led me off course.

To What or to Whom Are You Submitting Your Life?

This kind of mindset of purpose must be part of our nature if we are to succeed in everything we do. In the case of Jesus, He was not only determined, but He focused on that which was His responsibility to the Father, recognizing the work of the Father in relation to Himself. In John 6:37-39, He said:

"Everything that the Father gives Me will come to Me, and the one who comes to Me I certainly will not cast out. For I have come down from heaven, not to do My own will, but the will of Him who sent Me. And this is the will of Him who sent Me, that of everything that He has given Me I will lose nothing, but will raise it up on the last day."

How much of our plans are directly tied to what Christ is doing here in the world that we live in? Jesus was working very closely in connection to what the Father was doing and fulfilling His responsibility to the Father. Do we present our business ideas, life schedules, or ministries to Jesus, asking Him to partner with us or join our venture, when actually it should be the other way around? Should we not find out what He has sent us to do and then work everything else around that? I believe this was the mindset of Christ. Look at this further in John 8:29: "And *He who sent Me* is with Me; He has not left Me alone, *for I always do* the things that are pleasing to Him."

What are the things we do that please Christ who has sent us on His mission? It was not, "I'll try to do it," "I aim to do it," "I'll do my best," or "I'll do it some of the time or most of the time." It was specifically, "I always do."

SENT...

WHAT ARE THE THINGS WE DO THAT PLEASE CHRIST WHO HAS SENT US ON HIS MISSION? IT WAS NOT, "I'LL TRY TO DO IT," "I AIM TO DO IT," "I'LL DO MY BEST," OR "I'LL DO IT SOME OF THE TIME OR MOST OF THE TIME." IT WAS SPECIFICALLY, "I ALWAYS DO."

We have the same resource of Christ's presence: "Teaching them to follow all that *I* commanded *you*; and behold, *I am with you* always, to the end of the age" (Matthew 28:20).

Here we have specific orders. But that's not all. As I just stated, there is the promise of His presence being with us in the same manner that the Father's presence was with Him. We also see this same principle applied throughout John 14:19-21 which teaches us about love as the basis of a relationship:

"After a little while the world will no longer see Me, but you will see Me; because I live, you will live also. In that day you will know that I am in My Father, and you in Me, and I in you. He who has My commandments and keeps them is the one who loves Me; and he who loves Me will be loved by My Father, and I will love him and will disclose Myself to him."

Over and over again, Jesus, coupled with position and relationship with the Father, set the stage of His mindset and urgency of purpose. See John 9:4: "We must carry out the *works of Him who sent Me* as long as it is day; night is coming, when no one can work." It was not His own works. It was the works of "Him who sent Me." In relation to the works of God, an interesting story about Jesus at the well in Samaria and His discourse is found in John 4:31-34:

Meanwhile the disciples were urging Him, saying, "Rabbi, eat something." But He said to them, "I have food to eat that you do not know about." So the disciples were saying to one another, "No one brought Him anything to eat, did he?" Jesus said to them, "My food is to do the will of Him who sent Me and to accomplish His work."

Before we can speak here of the "work" which is of vast importance, there is the element of priority and importance. Jesus made this remark with specific intensity in this story. He said, "Hey, what's more important than food?" I remember being a kid on the farm during haying season. There were so many days of sunshine and good weather, and that was the time to cut the hay, dry it, and put it into the barn. On those hot days, we kids would glance down toward the Saint John River, flowing lazily by as if not a care in the world. Its cool, glistening waters sparkled and solicited a luring invitation to jump in for a refreshing swim. Yet a look of surprise would emerge on my dad's face, with raised eyebrows, if even a hint of this temptation was on our lips.

He would remark, "Don't even think of it! Tonight, after your work is all done, then help yourself to all the swimming you want, but until then, we have work to do!"

So much for that! The all-important work of getting the hay in would override any suggestion of taking to the cool waters. And speaking of food, it was even brought out to us in the field so that we wouldn't have to go back to the farm house for a meal and waste any time on work. Again, at night, when the day was over

SENT...

and the dew was settling, we had the luxury of sitting around the kitchen table to enjoy a hot meal at haying time.

There was a similar intensity and urgency to the mission Jesus was on this day when He encountered the Samaritan lady at the well. I do not think this meeting at the well happened by chance. I think Jesus knew His mission well before He even set out on His journey that day to pass through Samaria—it was His very purpose.

When the disciples returned from buying food in the city, they said to Jesus in verse 31, "Rabbi, eat," but Jesus answered with an unusual reply in verse 32: "I have food to eat that you do not know about."

> **THERE WAS A DIFFERENT DIMENSION TO CHRIST'S VERY PURPOSE, HIS VERY DRIVE, AND HIS MISSION'S IMPORTANCE— IT WAS MUCH MORE ESSENTIAL THAN THE FOOD WE CONSUME.**

In other words, "You don't have any idea of the food I have!" There was a different dimension to Christ's very purpose, His very drive, and His mission's importance—it was much more essential than the food we consume. And of course, we all know what is much more important than food! The disciples were thinking on exactly that level in verse 33, "So the disciples were saying to one another, 'No one brought Him *anything* to eat, did he?'"

It was not wrong to think that—absolutely not! They were thinking, *Who bought Him the "hamburger" while we were in town buying groceries?!* Very logical, right?

Then Jesus answered full of passion and zeal in verse 34: "My food is to do *the will of Him who sent Me* and *to accomplish His work.*"

And here we have it, loud and clear—the food He was talking about in His mindset of purpose—the food that exceeds all natural desire, surpassing physical need or fulfillment, in the spirit of submission and Godly initiative! Clearly, His food was to do the will of "Him who sent Me!" His food was also "to accomplish His work." Note it wasn't "my work," nor "my idea or desire," not even "my project," but clearly "His work." It was the work of the Father Jesus was sent to do. This was Christ's mindset and purpose.

So, then what was His work or the work of the Father? John 6:29 says, "Jesus answered and said to them, 'This is the *work of God*, that you *believe in Him whom He has sent.*'" This was the message of hope and salvation that we will cover in more detail later on. This was the gospel of Christ, which is the theme of our mission and the message of Christ.

Like an explosion, as if diverting from the text itself, Jesus made a profound declaration about the great mission, a statement that so many are familiar with: "Do you not say, 'There are still four months, and *then* comes the harvest? Behold, I tell you, raise your eyes and observe the fields, that they are white for harvest'" (John 4:35).

Here, we are given the keys to evangelism, missions, and the work of the kingdom for harvest within the context of the very will and purpose of the Father. Of course, the harvest was taking place right then and there, as the Father had determined for Jesus. Would He send Him anywhere else? When we read the rest of the chapter and the story of the woman and her town in

SENT...

Samaria, we realize why Jesus was so consumed to do the "will of Him who sent Me" and to "accomplish His work," even above the desire to eat food.

No wonder He started out his next exposition with the words, "Do you not say, 'There are yet four months, and *then* comes the harvest?'" The harvest is where the "will of the Father" is being done! It is happening right now as we do the will of God.

I honestly get troubled when I listen to those who are always talking about a "coming revival." Often, their prayers consist of praying for revival and looking forward to the day when the harvest will happen! They pray as if it will take place someday, sometime in the future—like "yet four months, and then comes the harvest." Even more disgusting are these prayers, "God, please start doing something!" or "God, start moving!" What a shame—as if God has a hard time getting things going and needs our coaxing and begging to get things started on His end. That is an insult to the supremacy of God Almighty. We do not send God, but Christ is He who sends us! Again, John 20:21 very clearly states, "So Jesus said to them again, 'Peace to you! As the Father has sent Me, I also send you.'"

> **CHRIST, BY THE POWER OF THE HOLY SPIRIT, IS ALWAYS ON THE MOVE, DEALING WITH MANKIND, WORKING ENDLESSLY IN SUPREME DOMINANCE AND SOVEREIGNTY, AND DIRECTING EVERY ASPECT OF HIS KINGDOM.**

Christ, by the power of the Holy Spirit, is always on the move, dealing with mankind, working endlessly in supreme dominance

To What or to Whom Are You Submitting Your Life?

and sovereignty, and directing every aspect of His kingdom. He directly sends us and charges us with His doing, His activity, and His harvest. He is always ready, moving, and doing. The question is, are we? The questions following closely behind are, how and when?

Are we those who are echoing the harvest will take place in four months? Are we praying endless, useless hours for the revival to happen, when the harvest is here now, exactly when and where He has "Sent . . ." us. He is the sender, and He well knows when and where to send us! He does not send us where there is nothing or to harvest in the middle of winter! He does not send us to an empty field of rocks or into a snow storm to bring in a harvest! Why are our efforts sometimes so unfruitful? Might it be that we have determined by our own will—perhaps by circumstances, finances, or some influence other than Christ's will—to send ourselves on an errand or mission that brings little harvest, if any. In this statement, Christ stated clearly in John 4:35: "Behold, I say to you, raise your eyes and observe the fields, that they are white for harvest."

There is no lack of harvest. Altogether, it may be a lack of our understanding of timing, location, place, or purpose because of where we have chosen to go, or what we have chosen to do and when, instead of going and doing what He has sent us for and when and where He has sent us to do it. No matter how well or poorly we have built our lives, ambitions, and goals, if not commissioned by Him, we have very little to show for them when it is all said and done. In 1 Corinthians 3:11-13 (WE), Paul taught:

> For no other foundation can anyone lay than that which is laid, which is Jesus Christ. Now if anyone builds on this foundation with gold, silver, precious stones, wood, hay, straw, each one's work will become clear; for the Day will

SENT...

declare it, because it will be revealed by fire; and the fire will test each one's work, of what sort it is.

Finally, within the context of His own actions, having been sent of the Father, Jesus gave us explicit instructions and explanations in John 4: 36-38:

> *"Already the one who reaps is receiving wages and is gathering fruit for life eternal; so that the one who sows and the one who reaps may rejoice together. For in this case the saying is true, 'One sows and another reaps.' I sent you to reap that for which you have not labored; others have labored, and you have come into their labor."*

Christ here said again, "I send you," and by the work of the Holy Spirit, He knows quite well what He is doing across all the earth. He is quite capable of looking after the affairs of His kingdom. He simply needs His servants, His laborers, to go and do as they are instructed according to His command, leadership, resources, and timing, submitted and obedient to Him. That is why He said in Matthew 9:38, "Therefore plead with the *Lord of the harvest to send out* workers into *His harvest.*"

He is the Lord of the harvest. He is the one who sends, and when it is all said and done, it is His harvest. We are the ones who are there at His bidding.

> **HE IS THE LORD OF THE HARVEST. HE IS THE ONE WHO SENDS, AND WHEN IT IS ALL SAID AND DONE, IT IS HIS HARVEST. WE ARE THE ONES WHO ARE THERE AT HIS BIDDING.**

This is the determined mindset of purpose Christ was focused on throughout His entire ministry on earth.

ATTITUDE OF SUBMISSION AND INITIATIVE

Jesus was so dependent on the Father and in such total submission that the things Jesus spoke and did were entirely wrapped up and enveloped with the very words and thoughts of the Father, and these He expressed as He spoke and did what He did. Jesus expressed Himself as totally limited and inadequate without the Father to whom His life was utterly submitted"

> *Therefore Jesus answered and was saying to them, "Truly, truly, I say to you, the Son can do nothing of Himself, unless it is something He sees the Father doing; for whatever the Father does, these things the Son also does in the same way. —John 5:19*

He said it over and over again:

> *"I can do nothing on My own initiative. As I hear, I judge; and My judgment is just, because I do not seek My own will, but the will of Him who sent Me." —John 5:30*

Again, Jesus was totally submitted, not only in His actions in doing the will of the Father, but He was dedicated to the very words and thoughts of His Father. John 7:28-29 states:

> *Then Jesus cried out in the temple, teaching and saying, "You both know Me and know where I am from; and I have not come of Myself, but He who sent Me is true, whom you do not know. I know Him, because I am from Him, and He sent Me.*

SENT...

Jesus strongly applied the fact that He was sent not only with words of tribute to the Father, which He so often did, but with His entire life, exemplifying an attitude of submission to the Father.

> **JESUS STRONGLY APPLIED THE FACT THAT HE WAS SENT NOT ONLY WITH WORDS OF TRIBUTE TO THE FATHER, WHICH HE SO OFTEN DID, BUT WITH HIS ENTIRE LIFE, EXEMPLIFYING AN ATTITUDE OF SUBMISSION TO THE FATHER.**

After the whole episode of the woman caught in adultery in John 8, Jesus made His defense strong under the authority of whom He is acting and doing. We have referred to many scriptures that illustrate this. In the same chapter, verse 28, Jesus continued, "When you lift up the Son of Man, then you will know that I am, and *I do nothing on My own, but I say these things as the Father instructed Me.*"

Yet, the Jews tried to qualify themselves by answering Him in this way:

> *So Jesus was saying to those Jews who had believed Him, "If you continue in My word, then you are truly My disciples; and you will know the truth, and the truth will set you free." They answered Him, "We are Abraham's descendants and have never yet been enslaved to anyone; how is it that You say, 'You will become free?'" ... I know that you are Abraham's descendants; yet you are seeking to kill Me, because My word has no place for you. I speak of the things which I have seen with My Father; therefore*

> *you also do the things which you heard from your father.*
> —*John 8:31-33, 37-38*

The Jews continued to argue in verse 39: "They answered and said to Him, 'Abraham is our father.' Jesus said to them, "If you are Abraham's children, do the deeds of Abraham.'"

Jesus continued His response to them:

> *Jesus said to them, "If God were your Father, you would love Me, for I proceeded forth and have come from God, for I have not even come on My own initiative, but He sent Me. Why do you not understand what I am saying? It is because you cannot hear My word.* —*John 8:42-43*

To say the least, Jesus got right to the point in no diplomatic way when He replied in John 8:44-45:

> *"You are of your father the devil, and you want to do the desires of your father. He was a murderer from the beginning, and does not stand in the truth because there is no truth in him. Whenever he tells a lie, he speaks from his own nature, because he is a liar and the father of lies."*

That is putting it pretty straight! Jesus continued in verse 47, "The one who is of God hears the words of God; for this reason you do not hear them, because you are not of God."

Of course, the Jews were not going to let Jesus off the hook, so they turned on Him with accusations such as, "Do we not say rightly that You are a Samaritan and have a demon?" (John 8:48) to which Jesus replied:

> *"I do not have a demon; on the contrary, I honor My Father, and you dishonor Me. But I am not seeking My glory; there is One who seeks it, and judges. Truly, truly*

SENT...

I say to you, if anyone follows My word, he will never see death. —John 8:49-51

This only infuriated the Jews more and they bombarded and barraged Him with accusations that He had a demon, "You are not greater than our father Abraham, who died, are You? The prophets died too. Whom do You make Yourself out to be?" (v. 53)

In other words, the Jews were saying, "Who do you think you are!" Jesus simply answered them in verses 54 and 55 by stating:

"If I glorify Myself, My glory is nothing; it is My Father who glorifies Me, of whom you say, 'He is our God'; and you have not come to know Him, but I know Him. And if I say that I do not know Him, I will be a liar like you; but I do know Him, and I follow His word."

Jesus added more and finally said in verse 58: "Truly, truly I say to you, before Abraham was born, I am." This brought the Jews to a point of such furious anger that "They picked up stones to throw at Him, but Jesus hid Himself and left the temple grounds" (verse 59).

> **JESUS RECOGNIZED THAT THERE IS BUT ONE SOURCE THAT HE, AS WELL AS ALL OF US, HAVE WHEN WE STAY IN SUBMISSION AND DRAW FROM GOD HIMSELF IN ALL WE DO AND SAY.**

This simply and very explicitly shows to us the extent of Jesus's commitment to not only say the words He was commissioned to say, but He also recognized that there is but one source that He, as well as all of us, have when we stay in submission and draw from

To What or to Whom Are You Submitting Your Life?

God Himself in all we do and say. It is a powerful illustration of what motivated Him, and in turn, should motivate us!

The scriptures continue to be poured out in the following chapters, where Jesus comes back to these truths repeatedly, demonstrating His attitude of total submission and initiative. In John 12:49, Jesus says, "For I did not speak on My own, but the *Father Himself who sent Me has given Me a commandment as to what to say* and what to speak."

Jesus was totally submitted to the Father, and therefore, to the purpose for which He was sent. He never questioned it. Even His initiative and authority came from the commandment of the Father:

> *"For this reason the Father loves Me, because I lay down My life so that I may take it back. No one has taken it away from Me, but I lay it down on My own. I have authority to lay it down, and I have authority to take it back. This commandment I received from My Father.* —John 10:17-18

John 14:31 says, "But so that the world may know that I love the Father, *I do exactly as the Father commanded Me.* Get up, let's go from here." Then, we see a series of scriptures that drive this point home. In John 17:3-4, Jesus says, "And this is eternal life, that they may know You, the only true God, and Jesus Christ *whom You have sent.* I glorified You on the earth by accomplishing *the work which You have given Me to do.*"

We see in John 13:16, "Truly, truly I say to you, *a slave is not greater than his master,* nor *is one who is sent greater than the one who sent him.*" John 14:28 states, "You heard that I said to you, 'I am going away, and I am coming to you.' If you loved Me, you

SENT...

would have rejoiced because *I am going to the Father, for the Father is greater than I.*"

Echoing this truth, Jesus adds, "Do you not believe that I am in the Father, and the Father is in Me? The words that I say to you I do not *speak on My own, but the Father, as He remains in me, does His works*" (John 14:10).

If there was ever a time in the life of Christ, a moment He may have even flinched in doing the will of God, it may have been the moment in the garden of Gethsemane at the Mount of Olives when even an angel from heaven came to strengthen Him. It was the moment He prayed, "Father, if You are willing, remove this cup from Me; yet *not My will*, but *Yours be done*" (Luke 22:42).

> **IF THERE WAS EVER A TIME IN THE LIFE OF CHRIST, A MOMENT HE MAY HAVE EVEN FLINCHED IN DOING THE WILL OF GOD, IT MAY HAVE BEEN THE MOMENT IN THE GARDEN OF GETHSEMANE.... BUT HE FELL BACK INTO TOTAL SUBMISSION AND UTTERED, "YET NOT MY WILL, BUT YOURS BE DONE."**

It is as if He were saying, "Father, if in any way possible, there is even a chance You may reconsider—maybe put plan B into effect, would you do it?" But then as quickly as He made this statement, hardly without a pause, He fell back into total submission and uttered, "Yet *not My will*, but *Yours be done.*"

Here we have the undeniable truth of the total obedience and submission to the will of the Father, Who had "Sent..." Him.

To What or to Whom Are You Submitting Your Life?

In the story of Him washing the feet of the disciples, Jesus exemplifies this attitude not only through words, but by example through servanthood and submission.

John 13:12-17, 20 relates the story:

Then, when He had washed their feet, and taken His garments and reclined at the table again, He said to them, "Do you know what I have done for you? You call Me 'Teacher' and 'Lord'; and you are correct, for so I am. So if I, the Lord and the Teacher, washed your feet, you also ought to wash one another's feet. For I gave you an example, so that you also would do just as I did for you. Truly, truly I say to you, a slave is not greater than his master, nor is one who is sent greater than the one who sent him. If you know these things, you are blessed if you do them. Truly, truly I say to you, the one who receives anyone I send, receives Me; and the one who receives Me receives Him who sent Me."

This is who He was. It was not just a demonstration of humility and submission. He was in total submission. He says, "For I gave you an example that *you also should do* as I did to you."

I hope we can go beyond the act of submission and catch the principle of what is being said. I have participated in some very great "foot washing" services in my time, so to speak. It comes from the fact that it was a custom in those days, due to the sandals they wore and the dirt roads they traveled on. We do not have that custom in our day and age. Though the custom is no longer alive, it can be followed symbolically by those who wish. I see no harm in it.

SENT...

It is the principle set forth that is much more important. In no way should it be overlooked; it should be practiced. Without dispute, this principle is that we should be servants one to another; we should serve each other in humility and with respect. And if this is the case with each other, then how much more important is it to submit to Christ Himself? When we do this, we are submitting and serving the Father who sent Him. Jesus is setting forth an extremely important principle in verse 16: "Truly, truly I say to you, *a slave is not greater than his master*, nor is one who is sent greater than the one who sent him."

Now, taking into account that Jesus understood that He was specifically "sent of the Father," He also repeatedly emphasized, like in this passage (v. 20): "Truly, truly I say to you, the one who receives anyone I send, receives Me; and the one who receives Me receives Him who sent Me."

Here, Jesus recognized that the Father was greater than Himself, and that was why Jesus saw Himself in submission to Him. He continued to make a very clear statement about this in John 14:28: "You heard that I said to you, 'I am going away, and I am coming to you.' If you loved Me, you would have rejoiced because I am going to the *Father*, for the *Father is greater than I*." He is clearly stating that since He was sent of the Father, the Father is the greater One, and therefore, Jesus was submitted to Him.

In fact, He says in the middle of it all in John 13:17: "If you know these things, you are blessed if you do them." In other words—the blessing of submission. It is the very heart of what Jesus lived in relation to the Father. I could write a whole volume on the subject. It is a powerful blessing to live out a life in such submission. It becomes a life filled with adventure and rewards as we walk with Christ with the attitude of submission to Him and with an initiative from Him.

CHAPTER 5

WHOSE PROMOTIONAL PACKAGE ARE YOU UNLOADING?

HEARING FROM HEAVEN

We start this chapter with John 8:50, "But I am not seeking My glory; there is One who seeks it, and judges." In this world, there are an immense number of promotional packages. Advertisements are such a huge part of our society. Billions upon billions are spent on advertising that not only gets the message

SENT...

out there, but competes for the attention of people, luring them to respond, most of which is primarily aimed at the pocket books of their target audiences.

Churches on evangelistic outreaches and missions work sometimes fall into the swing of things, aiming to get the needed support to complete the cause or mission. That is not all bad. Not all advertising is bad. There is a lot of valuable information that travels out over the airwaves and printed pages that is very useful to us in getting the things we need and enjoy having. Neither is that bad.

Preaching and proclaiming the gospel is part of God's plan. Jesus did this Himself. Luke 8:1 says: "Soon afterward, Jesus *began* going around from one city and village to another, proclaiming and *preaching the kingdom* of God. The twelve were with Him."

Christ followers did this. Acts 8:12 says, "But when they believed Philip as he was *preaching the good news about the kingdom of God and the name of Jesus Christ*, both men and women were being baptized."

Paul the apostle traveled extensively and preached, "And now, behold, I know that all of you, among whom I went about *preaching the kingdom*, will no longer see my face" (Acts 20:25). Further, Acts 28:30-31 says, "Now Paul stayed two full years in his own rented lodging and welcomed all who came to him, preaching the kingdom of God and teaching things about the Lord Jesus Christ with all openness, unhindered."

> **THERE IS NO END TO THE PROCLAMATION OF THE GOSPEL AND KINGDOM OF GOD, EVEN TO THIS DAY.**

Whose Promotional Package Are You Unloading?

There is no end to the proclamation of the gospel and kingdom of God, even to this day. For some time now, this proclamation has also been made across many media avenues, like printed materials, radio, and television. Of late, the internet has exploded, modernizing communications to an unimaginable level. There is no end to the possibilities of how the proclamation of the message of the kingdom can be communicated. Who could have imagined all of this would be possible, not to mention, what is yet to come. Never before has there been a time so opportune for spreading of gospel. Wise are those who use these means to spread the news of Christ.

Yet, in the enthusiasm of our activity, we can quickly divert to our own message, our cause, our ideas of others, our traditions, and our expectations of others. Before we know it, unrecognizable to us, we drift way off track, not listening at all to the words of Christ in our hearts but racing off with inventions of our own. Matthew 7:15 says, "Beware of the *false prophets*, who come to you in sheep's clothing, but inwardly are ravenous wolves."

In Matthew 16, Christ warns of this kind of false teaching three times:

> *And Jesus said to them, "Watch out and beware of the leaven of the Pharisees and Sadducees. How is it that you do not understand that I did not speak to you about bread? But beware of the leaven of the Pharisees and Sadducees." Then they understood that He did not say to beware of the leaven of bread, but of the teaching of the Pharisees and Sadducees. —Matthew 16:6 and 11-12*

I will not go into their teachings, but just like they had them then, so we have them today.

SENT...

Paul also warned against them just as Jesus did in Titus 1:10-14:
For there are many rebellious people, empty talkers and deceivers, especially those of the circumcision, who must be silenced because they are upsetting whole families, teaching things they should not teach for the sake of dishonest gain. One of them, a prophet of their own, said, "Cretans are always liars, evil beasts, lazy gluttons." This testimony is true. For this reason reprimand them severely so that they may be sound in the faith, not paying attention to Jewish myths and commandments of men who turn away from the truth.

And more in Colossians 2:19-22:
Not holding firmly to the head, from whom the entire body, being supplied and held together by the joints and ligaments, grows with a growth which is from God. If you have died with Christ to the elementary principles of the world, why, as if you were living in the world, do you submit yourself to decrees, such as, "Do not handle, do not taste, do not touch!" (which all refer to things destined to perish with use)—in accordance with the commandments and teachings of men?

Sooner or later, we all eventually run across those who have become diverters of the message of the gospel of the kingdom or promoters of themselves, their organization, their church—zealous but not hearing as Jesus heard who kept Himself aligned with the words of the Father.

We have studied in depth, and see quite clearly, that Jesus was sent and commissioned and now He does the same for us. But now, let's ask Jesus the question at hand. What was He promoting and where did he get his information? Listen to Jesus in John 7:14-18:

> *But when it was now the middle of the feast, Jesus went up into the temple area, and began to teach. The Jews then were astonished, saying, "How has this man become learned, not having been educated?" So Jesus answered them and said, "My teaching is not My own, but His who sent Me. If anyone is willing to do His will, he will know about the teaching, whether it is of God, or I am speaking from Myself. The one who speaks from himself seeks his own glory; but He who is seeking the glory of the One who sent Him, He is true, and there is no unrighteousness in Him."*

Quite straightforward. And Jesus, the Son of God, said this. Then how much more should we "hear from heaven"—the words of the Holy Spirit—in our inner most being?

> *"I have many things to speak and to judge regarding you, but He who sent Me is true; and the things which I heard from Him, these I say to the world." They did not realize that He was speaking to them about the Father. So Jesus said, "When you lift up the Son of Man, then you will know that I am, and I do nothing on My own, but I say these things as the Father instructed Me."* —John 8:26-28

What a statement, what an insight, understanding, and revelation of the key of Christ's spoken message, not to mention His actions! Christ was in constant communication with the Father—hearing from Heaven, so to speak. He listened for what He should say, what He should teach, and what He should do. Was it really that intense? Indeed, it must have been when He not once, but

SENT...

many times, repeated on numerous occasions, "I do nothing on My own, *but I speak these things as the Father instructed Me.*"

Jesus hammers His message home, leaving no doubt of His connection to hearing His Father. His message came directly from the term, "from heaven!" You couldn't get much more specific than this when you read what Jesus was saying. It is pretty powerful, to say the least: "For I did not speak on My own, *but the Father Himself who sent Me has given Me a commandment as to what to say and what to speak.*" John 14:24 says, "The one who does not love Me does not follow My words; and *the word which you hear is not Mine, but the Father's who sent Me.*"

In John 17:8, we see, "For *the words which You gave Me* I have given to them; and they received them and truly understood that *I came forth from You, and they believed that You sent Me.*"

John 3:34 says, "For *He whom God has sent* speaks the words of God; for He does not give the Spirit sparingly."

Therefore, Jesus goes on to explain:

"For the Father loves the Son and shows Him all things that He Himself is doing; and the Father will show Him greater works than these, so that you will be amazed. For just as the Father raises the dead and gives them life, so the Son also gives life to whom He wishes. For not even the Father judges anyone, but He has given all judgment to the Son, so that all will honor the Son even as they honor the Father. The one who does not honor the Son does not honor the Father who sent Him.

"Truly, truly, I say to you, the one who hears My word, and believes Him who sent Me, has eternal life, and does

not come into judgment, but has passed out of death into life." —John 5:20-24

I used to wonder years ago what Jesus had to pray for. Why would the Son of God have to *fight through* in prayer, travail, and warfare? He had it all, and I used to think and wonder why He needed to wait on the Father for anything. I did not realize what prayer was other than with persistence, getting something from God, trying to get God to do something that I thought was necessary, or bless me and my plans. How foolish I was! Now I understand it so differently. It is a love relationship—a communion and fellowship—it was hearing from the Father and learning and understanding the purposes and will of God being manifest through Him, through us. Prayer is sometimes more listening than speaking. It is so much more than speaking—a whole volume could be written in depth on this. Yet, now I understand why Jesus prayed so often. Matthew 14:23 tells us, "After He had sent the crowds away, He went up on the mountain by Himself to *pray*; and when it was evening, He was there alone."

PRAYER IS SOMETIMES MORE LISTENING THAN SPEAKING.

Luke 5:16 says, "But *Jesus* Himself would *often* slip away to the wilderness and *pray*." Again, Luke 6:12 remarks, "Now it was at this time that He went off to the mountain to *pray*, and He spent the whole night in *prayer* with God." Finally, Luke 9:18 states, "And it happened that while He was *praying* alone, the disciples were with Him, and He questioned them, saying, "Who do the people say that I am?"

SENT...

WHAT IS THE MESSAGE?

As messengers of the gospel—ministers of churches, presidents of Christian foundations, leaders of religious causes, trailblazers of missionary movements, home group leaders, music developers and song writers, housewives in small Bible study groups, leaders of men's faith advances, and the people who do hundreds and thousands of things in the name of God, what is the message? What is it that we are all saying, doing, and carrying out in our countless deeds? What message are we promoting? What and who are we promoting?

These are not words of condemnation, but a question. It is a question we ask ourselves more often than not before we get overambitious about what we are saying and doing. It is a question we should ask ourselves with deep conviction to bring us back to the theme of this book, which is laid out in John 20:21, "So Jesus said to them again, 'Peace be to you; just as the Father has sent Me, I also send you.'"

Would He Who sends us not have the answer to these questions? In the light of all that has been said up to now in this book, we are again brought back to the life of Christ and His perspective on His mission and His relationship with the message He promoted.

Let's go back to see what the message of Jesus was, where it came from, and what deeds it produced? Then, in light of fact that Jesus "sends us in like manner," we can examine the answer to the above questions we may ask ourselves.

First of all, Christ's message was one that came from His Father. Jesus's claim was clear in John 3:34: "For *He whom God sent speaks the words of God*; for He does not give the Spirit sparingly." So, in

Whose Promotional Package Are You Unloading?

the words of Christ (John 6:28-29), "Therefore they said to Him, 'What are we to do, so that we may accomplish the works of God?' Jesus answered and said to them, 'This is the work of God, that *you believe in Him whom He has sent.*'"

How did Jesus portray this? What was His message?

Jesus says this very clearly. It was a message of salvation, not judgement and condemnation. It was about salvation by and through Him.

Since the whole religious world of that time was pointing fingers of accusation, judging others, comparing one's achievement over the other people's, piously condemning those who did not add up, these were welcome words! As John 3:17 puts it, "For God did not *send the Son* into the world to judge the world, but that the world might be *saved through Him*."

This was the message for the hungry and thirsty: "Jesus said to them, '*I am the bread of life*; the one who comes to Me will not be hungry, and the one who believes in Me will *never be thirsty*'"(John 6:35).

The message was life in its fullest form, offered freely! Jesus warns and promises us (John 10:10), "The thief comes only to steal and kill and destroy; *I came so that they would have life, and have it abundantly*."

His was a transforming message of power that would change the very lives of people—spiritually, physically, mentally, and socially, from total darkness to total light! The whole works! John 12:46 says, "*I have come as Light into the world*, so that *no one who believes in Me* will remain in darkness."

Jesus promoted this by calling mankind to put their faith in Him: "The one who *believes in Him* is not judged; the one who

SENT...

does not believe has been judged already, because he has *not believed* in the *name of the only Son of God"* (John 3:18).

> **HIS WAS A TRANSFORMING MESSAGE OF POWER THAT WOULD CHANGE THE VERY LIVES OF PEOPLE—SPIRITUALLY, PHYSICALLY, MENTALLY, AND SOCIALLY, FROM TOTAL DARKNESS TO TOTAL LIGHT! THE WHOLE WORKS!**

Talk about "water" and "believing!" There is one particularly incredible story at the beginning of Jesus's ministry where He meets the Samaritan woman at the well on His way to Galilee. He speaks freely about giving her "living water" in John 4:10: "If you knew the gift of God, and who it is who is saying to you, 'Give Me a drink,' you would have asked Him, and He would have given you living water."

There are many aspects and truths in this story, but to stick to the point, Jesus continues to expound to her, in spite of her "not getting it" initially:

> *Jesus answered and said to her, "Everyone who drinks of this water will be thirsty again; but whoever drinks of the water that I will give him shall never thirst; but the water that I will give him will become in him a fountain of water springing up to eternal life." —John 4:13-14*

She still did not get it, but this does not deter Jesus in any way.

A fantastic story of a man born blind is recorded in John 9. The whole story is well worth our attention and much could be

Whose Promotional Package Are You Unloading?

said and learned from it, but I am bringing just one excerpt to your attention:

> He answered by saying, "And who is He, Sir, that I may believe in Him?" Jesus said to him, "You have both seen Him, and He is the one who is talking with you." And he said, "I believe, Lord." And he worshiped Him. —John 9:36-38

You may even note that he was made well even before he believed. The end result was that he believed and worshiped Him—the Pharisees didn't. They had their own message; they had their own promotional package to unload.

In fact, John tells quite the story after Jesus delivered the message in the first part of the chapter about being the Good Shepherd. I think it is worth reading:

> "Truly, truly I say to you, the one who does not enter by the door into the fold of the sheep, but climbs up some other way, he is a thief and a robber. But the one who enters by the door is a shepherd of the sheep. To him the doorkeeper opens, and the sheep listen to his voice, and he calls his own sheep by name and leads them out. When he puts all his own sheep outside, he goes ahead of them, and the sheep follow him because they know his voice. However, a stranger they simply will not follow, but will flee from him, because they do not know the voice of strangers." Jesus told them this figure of speech, but they did not understand what the things which He was saying to them meant.
>
> So Jesus said to them again, "Truly, truly I say to you, I am the door of the sheep. All those who came before Me

SENT...

are thieves and robbers, but the sheep did not listen to them. I am the door; if anyone enters through Me, he will be saved, and will go in and out and find pasture. The thief comes only to steal and kill and destroy; I came so that they would have life, and have it abundantly.

I am the good shepherd; the good shepherd lays down His life for the sheep. He who is a hired hand, and not a shepherd, who is not the owner of the sheep, sees the wolf coming, and leaves the sheep and flees; and the wolf snatches them and scatters the flock. He flees because he is a hired hand and does not care about the sheep. I am the good shepherd, and I know My own, and My own know Me, just as the Father knows Me and I know the Father; and I lay down My life for the sheep. And I have other sheep that are not of this fold; I must bring them also, and they will listen to My voice; and they will become one flock, with one shepherd. For this reason the Father loves Me, because I lay down My life so that I may take it back. No one has taken it away from Me, but I lay it down on My own. I have authority to lay it down, and I have authority to take it back. This commandment I received from My Father." —John 10:1-18

This, of course, did not sit well with one group of listeners but others were thinking about it seriously in John 10:19-21:

Dissension occurred again among the Jews because of these words. Many of them were saying, "He has a demon and is insane. Why do you listen to Him?" Others were saying, "These are not the words of one who is demon-possessed. A demon cannot open the eyes of those who are blind, can it?"

Much could be said about this fantastic exposition of Jesus, but let's follow Him as He pushes back on their resistance at the Feast of Dedication and on the portico of Solomon in verse 24: "The Jews then surrounded Him and began saying to Him, 'How long will You keep us in suspense? If You are the Christ, tell us plainly.'"

Then Jesus gets right to the point:

Jesus answered them, "I told you, and you do not believe; the works that I do in My Father's name, these testify of Me. But you do not believe, because you are not of My sheep. My sheep listen to My voice, and I know them, and they follow Me; and I give them eternal life, and they will never perish; and no one will snatch them out of My hand. My Father, who has given them to Me, is greater than all; and no one is able to snatch them out of the Father's hand. I and the Father are one." —John 10:25-30

The passage tells us that the Jews got so angry about Jesus's claim of His connection to the Father that they were grasping for rocks to stone Him. He managed to refute them further:

"If I do not do the works of My Father, do not believe Me; but if I do them, though you do not believe Me, believe the works, so that you may know and understand that the Father is in Me, and I in the Father." —John 10:37-38

Obviously, that did not help the Jews, as the Bibles says in verse 39, "Therefore they were seeking again to arrest Him, and He eluded their grasp."

SENT...

In other words, Jesus escaped them. Yet, the chapter ends with a short but beautiful truth in verse 42: "And many *believed in Him* there."

And many other stories like this unfold all throughout scripture over and over again. In fact, in the very next chapter, in the dramatic setting of the death and resurrection of Lazarus, Jesus addresses Martha:

Jesus said to her, "I am the resurrection and the life; the one who believes in Me will live, even if he dies, and everyone who lives and believes in Me will never die. Do you believe this?" She said to Him, "Yes, Lord; I have believed that You are the Christ, the Son of God, and He who comes into the world." —John 11:25-27

And further down in verse 45, "Therefore many of the Jews who came to Mary, and saw what He had done, *believed in Him.*"

The message was loud and clear. It came straight out of the throne room of the Father, and Jesus did not divert from it! In John 17:18 Jesus says of the Father, "For the words which *You gave Me I have given to them*; and they received them and truly understood that *I came forth from You*, and *they believed that You sent Me.*"

> **THERE IS A JOINED, INTIMATE RELATIONSHIP BETWEEN THE FATHER AND THOSE WHO REALLY BELIEVE.**

This truth would create a joined, intimate relationship between the Father and those who really believed. This paralleled His own relationship with His Father. He continued to explain this in various ways. For example, John 6:48-51 is tied very closely to the symbolism of the rite of communion:

> *"I am the bread of life. Your fathers ate the manna in the wilderness, and they died. This is the bread which comes down out of heaven, so that one may eat from it and not die. I am the living bread that came down out of heaven; if anyone eats from this bread, he will live forever; and the bread also which I will give for the life of the world also is My flesh."*

But the Jews still did not get it, and still not many get it today. It is a spiritual union and not a physical one:

> *Then the Jews began to argue with one another, saying, "How can this man give us His flesh to eat?" So Jesus said to them, "Truly, truly, I say to you, unless you eat the flesh of the Son of Man and drink His blood, you have no life in yourselves. The one who eats My flesh and drinks My blood has eternal life, and I will raise him up on the last day. For My flesh is true food, and My blood is true drink. The one who eats My flesh and drinks My blood remains in Me, and I in him. Just as the living Father sent Me, and I live because of the Father, the one who eats Me, he also will live because of Me. This is the bread which came down out of heaven; not as the fathers ate and died; the one who eats this bread will live forever." —vv. 52-58*

Jesus does not at all slow down, but persists with the message of spiritual unity. Notice this parallel: "I live because of the Father, so the one who eats Me, he also will live because of Me." This is the unity of what ties us with Jesus in the same manner Jesus is tied

SENT...

to the Father. This is a spiritual union or the union of the Holy Spirit—the Spirit of God.

John 15:1-11 describes this union, as well:

"I am the true vine, and My Father is the vinedresser. Every branch in Me that does not bear fruit, He takes away; and every branch that bears fruit, He prunes it so that it may bear more fruit. You are already clean because of the word which I have spoken to you. Remain in Me, and I in you. Just as the branch cannot bear fruit of itself but must remain in the vine, so neither can you unless you remain in Me. I am the vine, you are the branches; the one who remains in Me and I in him bears much fruit, for apart from Me you can do nothing. If anyone does not remain in Me, he is thrown away like a branch and dries up; and they gather them and throw them into the fire and they are burned. If you remain in Me, and My words remain in you, ask whatever you wish, and it will be done for you. My Father is glorified by this, that you bear much fruit, and so prove to be My disciples. Just as the Father has loved Me, I also have loved you; remain in My love. If you keep My commandments, you will remain in My love; just as I have kept My Father's commandments and remain in His love. These things I have spoken to you so that My joy may be in you, and that your joy may be made full."

Let's point out a reference made earlier. Did you notice something familiar here when He said, "Apart from Me you can do nothing?" Remember, Jesus said in relation to His Father in John 5:19, "The Son can do nothing of Himself" and in John 5:30, "I can do nothing on My own," and then again in John 8:28, "I do nothing on My own." Did you notice the parallel? It is not so much about ability as it is relationship. Our ability flows out of relationship. Relationship is what redemption is all about.

> **OUR ABILITY FLOWS OUT OF RELATIONSHIP. RELATIONSHIP IS WHAT REDEMPTION IS ALL ABOUT.**

The message of the purpose of Christ's redemption and hope is further tied together with relationship, followed by obedience. It is all related to us in parallel with His own knowledge, love, and obedience to the Father. This is then passed on to our relationship with one another. This is all in the same text as He commands us to carry this forward on the strong basis of relationship, founded on love:

> "This is My commandment, that you love one another, just as I have loved you. Greater love has no one than this, that a person will lay down his life for his friends. You are My friends if you do what I command you. No longer do I call you slaves, for the slave does not know what his master is doing; but I have called you friends, because all things that I have heard from My Father I have made known to you. You did not choose Me but I chose you, and appointed you that you would go and bear fruit, and that your fruit would remain, so that whatever you ask of the Father in My name He may give to you. This I command you, that you love one another. —John 15:12-17

SENT...

Prior to this passage, we see John 13:34-35:
> "I am giving you a new commandment, that you love one another, just as I have loved you, that you also love one another. By this all people will know that you are My disciples, if you have love for one another."

> **HEAVEN IS NOT THE GOAL OF OUR MESSAGE, NOR IS IT AN ATTEMPT TO GET PEOPLE READY FOR HIS COMING.**

In the light of this, we begin to realize our message is not something of our own making. It is not even one that attempts to save man from damnation and destruction. It is not even an attempt to get people to live right. Heaven is not the goal of our message, nor is it an attempt to get people ready for His coming. Indeed, we do not ignore these, but it is not our core message. This is the result of the message. Our message is being reconciled to God by His redemption. Our message is one of coming into relationship with Christ and therefore into relationship with the God of this universe. We come into a relationship of love which leads us to obedience and service to God in this world. We become motivated by Christ and His life and love in and through us.

WHAT IS THE MOTIVATION?

A whole discussion erupts at the temple when the Pharisees confront Jesus in John 8:38: "I speak of the things which I have seen with *My* Father; therefore you also do the things which you heard from *your* father."

Whose Promotional Package Are You Unloading?

Jesus mindset is established. He knows who He is working with and where He gets His information from. Jesus is telling the Pharisees that they have a different source of information and are working on another side. They argued with Jesus, but Jesus, without any apology, hit the mark and cut to the very heart of the matter (quite boldly, to say the least):

They answered and said to Him, "Abraham is our father." Jesus said to them, "If you are Abraham's children, do the deeds of Abraham. But as it is, you are seeking to kill Me, a man who has told you the truth, which I heard from God; this Abraham did not do. You are doing the deeds of your father." They said to Him, "We were not born as a result of sexual immorality; we have one Father: God." Jesus said to them, "If God were your Father, you would love Me, for I came forth from God and am here, for I have not even come on My own, but He sent Me." —John 8:39-42

It might do well for us to take another look at where we get our information from and whose deeds we are going about doing. By whose "initiative" is our mindset and purpose being motivated, stirred, and inspired?

Jesus again gets very specific and upsettingly undiplomatic when he narrows it down to the heart of the matter in verses 43 and 44:

"Why do you not understand what I am saying? It is because you cannot hear My word. You are of your father the devil, and you want to do the desires of your father. He was a murderer from the beginning, and does not stand in the truth because there is no truth in him.

SENT...

Whenever he tells a lie, he speaks from his own nature, because he is a liar and the father of lies."

Alarming indeed, yet true.

Like before, Jesus showed and took true ownership of His message and His motivation behind this in John 7:16-18:

"My teaching is not My own, but His who sent Me. If anyone is willing to do His will, he will know about the teaching, whether it is of God, or I am speaking from Myself. The one who speaks from himself seeks his own glory; but He who is seeking the glory of the One who sent Him, He is true, and there is no unrighteousness in Him."

He was not motivated in any way to promote Himself; instead, he was interested only in sending the message that came from the teaching of the Father which promoted the "glory of the One who sent Him."

What is the real motive behind our message? Even subconsciously, the secret behind our motives can be cleverly disguised, leading us to believe we have the best intentions. Whose message, what message, and where are we promoting the message we preach, teach, or even live out in our daily lives? Once again, I humbly bow before the King of Kings and let Him examine me with His Holy Spirit; examine my intentions, expectations, and motivations.

Now, I do not assume any of us to be perfect and/or advocate getting caught up in a whirlwind of self-examination, causing us to eventually lose focus, become flustered, and fall into the trap of legalism and false humility. But it is possible to develop a steady consciousness of these facts. Creating a healthy approach to this can actually become an encouragement to us—a release of pressure and expectations that we and others may place upon our ministry and Christian living. We can drive ourselves nuts trying to impress ourselves and others, gain approval, and make us feel good about ourselves. It happens!

> **WE CAN DRIVE OURSELVES NUTS TRYING TO IMPRESS OURSELVES AND OTHERS, GAIN APPROVAL, AND MAKE US FEEL GOOD ABOUT OURSELVES. IT HAPPENS!**

Jesus had many things He wanted to say and discuss, but His emphasis was consistently on His source and motivation for living the way He lived, as John 8:26-28 depicts:

"I have many things to say and to judge regarding you, but He who sent Me is true; and the things which I heard from Him, these I say to the world.

So Jesus said, "When you lift up the Son of Man, then you will know that I am, and I do nothing on My own, but I say these things as the Father instructed Me."

Over and over, Jesus says that all of His motivation and information comes from the eternal source of the Father, "The one who does not love Me does not follow My words; and the word which you hear is not Mine, but the Father's who sent Me" (John 14:24).

BOWING TO THE EXPECTATION OF OTHERS

Coming from a different angle, we will again look at John 10, where Jesus addresses the pressure the Jews were applying to try and extract information about Jesus, all for the sake of their own curiosity:

SENT...

> At that time the Feast of the Dedication took place in Jerusalem; it was winter, and Jesus was walking in the temple area, in the portico of Solomon. The Jews then surrounded Him and began saying to Him, "How long will You keep us in suspense? If You are the Christ, tell us plainly." Jesus answered them, "I told you, and you do not believe; the works that I do in My Father's name, these testify of Me. But you do not believe because you are not of My sheep. My sheep listen to My voice, and I know them, and they follow Me; and I give them eternal life, and they will never perish; and no one will snatch them out of My hand. My Father, who has given them to Me, is greater than all; and no one is able to snatch them out of the Father's hand. I and the Father are one. —John 10:22-30

Talk about setting the record straight. Jesus, right here in the Jew's own religious territory, answers them without hesitation. He does not even say His sheep are His alone but that they have been given Him of the Father. He challenges them: "Try taking them out of My Hand, if you dare!" Then Jesus drives the last point home (in my own words), "By the way, just in case that is not enough for you to understand, let me add that I and the Father are actually one, anyhow!"

That did it, and the Jews really got mad about the whole thing, this time mad enough to want to kill Him:

> The Jews picked up stones again to stone Him. Jesus replied to them, "I showed you many good works from the Father; for which of them are you stoning Me?" The Jews answered Him, "We are not stoning you for a good

> work, but for blasphemy; and because You, being a man, make Yourself out to be God." Jesus answered them, "Has it not been written in your Law, 'I said, you are gods'? If he called them gods, to whom the word of God came (and the Scripture cannot be broken), do you say of Him, whom the Father sanctified and sent into the world, 'You are blaspheming,' because I said, 'I am the Son of God?'"
> — John 10:31-36

They refute Jesus by saying He was blaspheming, claiming to be the Son of God! Did Jesus back off in any way? Did He apologize or water down His own statements or back down from His stance? No, I see none of that. He just continued to push further, making His connection with the Father ever more precise:

> "If I do not do the works of My Father, do not believe Me; but if I do them, though you do not believe Me, believe the works, so that you may know and understand that the Father is in Me, and I in the Father." Therefore they were seeking again to arrest Him, and He eluded their grasp.

This did not cool down the atmosphere in any way—that is for sure! They wanted to grab Jesus physically and do whatever that would have followed, but Jesus escaped their grasp. He evaded their grasp but had not for a moment budged from His stand of who He was in relation to the Father—not for an instant did He bow down to the threats of His accusers.

This was not the first time Jesus's life was threatened. He had experienced this before and after this occasion, related to the same topic of being sent of His Father as earlier passages, He passionately cried out in John 7:28-32:

SENT...

Then Jesus cried out in the temple, teaching and saying, "You both know Me and you know where I am from; and I have not come of Myself, but He who sent Me is true, whom you do not know. I do know Him, because I am from Him, and He sent Me." So they were seeking to arrest Him; and yet no one laid his hand on Him, because His hour had not yet come. But many of the crowd believed in Him; and they were saying, "When the Christ comes, He will not perform more signs than those which this man has done, will He?" The Pharisees heard the crowd whispering these things about Him, and the chief priests and the Pharisees sent officers to arrest Him.

John 8:18-20 states:

So they were saying to Him, "Where is Your Father?" Jesus answered, "You know neither Me nor My Father; if you knew Me, you would know My Father also." These words He spoke in the treasury, as He taught in the temple area; and no one arrested Him, because His hour had not yet come.

Then, unbelievably, the issue arises again in the very same chapter in John 8:58-59: "Jesus said to them, 'Truly, truly I say to you, *before Abraham was born, I am.*' Therefore they *picked up stones* to throw at Him, but *Jesus hid Himself* and left the temple *grounds.*'"

The plans to kill Jesus advanced and He had to evade them:

So from that day on they planned together to kill Him. Therefore Jesus no longer continued to walk publicly among the Jews, but went away from there to the region near the wilderness, into a city called Ephraim; and there He stayed with the disciples.

Now the chief priests and the Pharisees had given orders that if anyone knew where He was, he was to report it, so that they might arrest Him. —John 11: 53-54, 57

Then again, in the next chapter (John 12:36), Jesus has to escape because of what He said, "'While you have the Light, believe in the Light, so that you may become sons of Light.' These things Jesus spoke, and He went away and hid from them."

Yet just before this Jesus, had felt the urgency to pray:

"Now My soul has become troubled; and what am I to say, 'Father, save Me from this hour?' But for this purpose I came to this hour. Father, glorify Your name." Then a voice came out of heaven: "I have both glorified it, and will glorify it again." —John 12:27-28

There's no doubt that when the going gets hard and our own souls are troubled, we wish to escape the clutches of the pressure on us, we also say with a sigh of lament, "What am I to say, 'Father, save Me from this hour?'" But, we must then proceed to conclude this same prayer with, "But for this purpose I came to this hour. Father, glorify Your name."

Are we going to jump the gun and resolve this like Peter did, with the sword? Some of us may feel very justified in doing so. We can always resort to the sword! It works very effectively, and the results were fast coming—especially the ear of Malchus, the high priest's slave. Yet this was not the answer Jesus was looking for, "So Jesus said to Peter, 'Put the sword into the sheath; the cup which the Father has given Me, am I not to drink it?'" (John 18:11)

SENT...

There was no question in the answer Jesus gave. Jesus could have said, "This is what I must do," or "This is the circumstance I'm in." No, it was very specific: "The cup which the *Father has given Me*, am I not to drink it?"

It was a resolute devotion to the One who had sent Him.

> **JESUS EXHIBITED A RESOLUTE DEVOTION TO THE ONE WHO HAD SENT HIM.**

Are we equally as passionately committed and unyielding to stick to what the Holy Spirit has put into our hearts concerning the vision, purpose, and revelation of Christ in our lives? I am not talking about being stubborn, tenacious, and hard to get along with. I do not believe this is what Jesus was about. But what I am talking about is having our hearts and minds so consumed with our identity in Christ and having His calling and purpose so interwoven into our lives in such a way that even the demons of hell can do very little to stop us.

Neither the crushing circumstances of life nor the cunning influence of people could distract us from that which burns in our hearts, having been "Sent..." by Christ. Though In Galatians 2:20, though Paul was speaking of his spiritual identity in Christ, it likely "spilled over" into his everyday choices and the decisions he made under the pressures of his circumstances and the people he encountered:

> *I have been crucified with Christ; and it is no longer I who live, but Christ lives in me; and the life which I now live in the flesh I live by faith in the Son of God, who loved me and gave Himself up for me.*

Considering our spiritual birth in Christ and His purpose in us, would this not constitute the very life of Christ in us, drawn into the very inner circle of Deity? John 17:21 says, "That they may all be one; just as You, Father, *are* in Me and I in You, that *they also may be in Us*, so that the world may believe that *You sent Me*."

Our very life and connection is with Christ. That is why Jesus uses the example in John 15:4-8:

> *"Remain in Me, and I in you. As the branch cannot bear fruit of itself but must remain in the vine, so neither can you unless you abide in Me. I am the vine, you are the branches; the one who remains in Me and I in him bears much fruit, for apart from Me you can do nothing. If anyone does not remain in Me, he is thrown away like a branch and dries up; and they gather them and throw them into the fire, and they are burned. If you remain in Me, and My words remain in you, ask whatever you wish, and it will be done for you. My Father is glorified by this, that you bear much fruit, and so prove to be My disciples."*

We will return to this again toward the conclusion of this book, but I needed to place it here to emphasize that the very harmony of purpose in life has its roots and identity in Christ and Him alone. It becomes my driving force and source of energy. I am motivated not by needs, people's opinions, my own interests, skills, nor achievements, but by the sheer will of Christ burning within.

> **THE VERY HARMONY OF PURPOSE IN LIFE HAS ITS ROOTS AND IDENTITY IN CHRIST AND HIM ALONE.**

SENT...

We see an example of this when it came to Jesus's own family in John 2:3-5:

> *When the wine ran out, the mother of Jesus said to Him, "They have no wine." And Jesus said to her, "What business do you have with me, woman? My hour has not yet come." His mother said to the servants, "Whatever He tells you, do it."*

Even Jesus, who was so close to His own mother, was very conscious of His appointed "time," and responded to her in this way. He had pressures with very close family:

> *For not even His brothers believed in Him. So Jesus said to them, "My time is not yet here, but your time is always ready. The world cannot hate you, but it hates Me because I testify about it, that its deeds are evil. Go up to the feast yourselves; I am not going up to this feast, because My time has not yet fully arrived." —John 7:5-8*

Neither Mary nor His brothers could thwart the timing of the Father that Jesus was so conscious of. I am not certain what transpired in the moments right after and how things were calculated in the mind of Jesus, but the fact was that He did instruct them to fill the water pots and He did go to the feast, though perhaps in a much different way than anticipated by brothers, as the Scripture indicates: "But when His brothers had gone up to the feast, then He Himself also went up, not publicly, but as *though in secret*" (John 7:10).

In any case, whatever Jesus thought and when and why He did what He did was without a doubt deeply affected by His thoughts focused on the right "time" being "fully come." He was not there to simply bow to Mary's wishes or the suggestions of His brothers

Whose Promotional Package Are You Unloading?

or the situation at hand. He was fully conscious in His own confession of the "time" which was to be "fully come." Yet, Mary did have the good will and understanding to at least back off enough to say, "Just at least do what He says," leaving it up to His divine direction and decision. That might be a lot more than what we are willing to do.

Can we submit totally to Him and say, "In any case, I will just do as He says." Or are we going to start a prayer meeting to convince God that He should do something in this situation, and in our prayers give a full list of instructions of how this should be carried out. How often I hear payers and whole prayer meetings where we spend most of the prayer time and our energy informing God of the situation at hand. Then we spell out what needs to be done, and in an ongoing long prayer, explain how it needs to be accomplished, when, where, and why! Next time, take a conscious, calculated note of your own prayers and see how much of them are being said in this manner.

Years ago, my own prayer life was revolutionized at that point and time, when I discovered I did just that in my prayers. I found praying to be a "real job." I was even taught that praying was hard work—a real task to accomplish. Indeed it was. It was really hard work "telling God" how to "run this universe"—why wouldn't it be?

It was during the charismatic revival of praise and worship during the early 80s that in my prayer time, I would "sneak" in some worship during my times of hard work at prayer. I found it rather refreshing to focus in on Christ and His sovereignty, grace, and His very person. I would sing with my understanding of praise and worship to Him. Then I would shift to a different

SENT...

level of singing to Him, not out of my own understanding, but in a language not known to myself—called an unknown tongue. It was a time of bathing in His presence.

As a result, it often seemed "heaven" came alive in my soul and spirit. I began to get a flood of ideas and thoughts that did not particularly come from any calculated, rational thinking of my own mind. At first, I misunderstood them to be interruptions and wayward thoughts, things I had to do and errands that needed attention. I thought these were "tricks" of the devil to interfere with my valuable prayer time. I then came up with an idea: to lay such thoughts to rest, I should write them down. That would help me leave them be so they would not continue to reoccur and thus disturb my time of prayer, praise, and worship.

The astounding thing I discovered was that as I followed these thoughts through and paid attention to them, writing them down became very productive, it brought about good results because they were very necessary things that required serious attention. At first, some of them seemed very bizarre and purely "worldly," especially during prayer. For example, while worshiping, I suddenly got the idea: *Your car needs an oil change—when did you last check it?* Unbelievable! As I jotted down a reminder and later checked it—indeed, it was time for an oil change!

Now, they weren't all of this nature, but the more I paid attention to what I heard, the more productive my whole life, ministry, and work became. I learned to fine-tune my praise and worship, and as a result, my hearing became better and better. This trained my focus, tuning me into the realm of the Spirit and the operation of the gifts of the Spirit. It became a revolution in my whole spiritual walk and life with Christ! I used to feel guilty at first "sneaking" time off from my prayer life to enjoy the upsurge of praise and worship during these times—almost like cheating on my prayer times. Hard to believe this now when I reflect back on it.

> **THE INVALUABLE LESSON I LEARNED WAS THAT AS I FOCUSED ON CHRIST, THE MORE I LEARNED TO LISTEN.**

The invaluable lesson I learned was that as I focused on Christ, the more I learned to listen. I learned to listen to what He had to say. I learned His thoughts and heard His answers, even to questions I hardly had time to ask. Thoughts of revelation flowed into my heart and mind. Often, during these times, scripture would come alive and I began to learn in a brand new way, transforming my walk with God! This, and much more, were the things I learned, perhaps similar to what His mother had learned and told the servants in John 2:5, "Whatever He says to you, do it."

My life was totally changed and would never be the same again. Part of this change, which had only continued to develop over the years, is why I write this book today. Perhaps I have learned like Mary; instead of informing Jesus of my current situation, I waited for Him to act on the information I have to offer Him. I now am willing to wait and let Him take the initiative. I simply make sure I am ready to act on the basis of this principle, "Whatever He says to you, do it."

This is not always as easy as it sounds. So many of us cry out to God, wanting Him to speak, wanting to hear from Him. But so often, we really just want to hear what we want to hear, not what

SENT...

He has to say. Often, we are pleading for and are ready to agree with what we want to hear and agree to. I have people come to me for prayer, "Have you a word from God for me?" They are waiting for something that would confirm their agenda, something to help them decide what and what not to do. It is a serious thing to hear from God, because the minute we do, we have a solemn obligation to be obedient in, "Whatever He says to you, do it."

Then the whole factor of obedience comes into play, submission to the purpose and will of Christ in our lives. This often comes with a price. It was the governing principle in the life of Jesus in His relationship with the Father.

This is what Jesus is so very clearly saying (John 5:30): "I can do *nothing on My own*. As I hear, I judge; and My judgment is righteous, because I do not seek *My own will but the will of Him who sent Me*." He says in John 6:38, "For I have come down from heaven, *not to do My own will, but the will of Him who sent Me*."

This is the reason Jesus tells his followers in Luke 9:23, "If anyone wishes to come after Me, he must deny himself, and *take up his cross* daily and follow Me."

This is one of the reasons that in the very same chapter, the following account is brought to our attention:

As they were going on the road, someone said to Him, "I will follow You wherever You go." And Jesus said to him, "The foxes have holes and the birds of the sky have nests, but the Son of Man has nowhere to lay His head." And He said to another, "Follow Me." But he said, "Lord, permit me first to go and bury my father." But He said to him, "Allow the dead to bury their own dead; but as for you, go and proclaim everywhere the kingdom of God." Another also said, "I will follow You, Lord; but first permit me to say goodbye to those at my home." But Jesus said to him, "No one, after putting his hand to the plow and looking back, is fit for the kingdom of God." —Luke 9:57-62

The idea again brings us to the very subject under discussion and the title of this chapter, "Whose Promotional Package Are You Unloading?" Also remember this subtitle, "Bowing to the Expectation of Others."

It is a dying to self. It is a dying to the expectations that others and circumstances may be exacting on us. This is why He says in John 12:24: "Truly, truly I say to you, unless a *grain of wheat* falls into the earth and dies, it remains alone; but if it *dies*, it bears much fruit."

But in all of this there is a bigger picture, a much greater side. There is the side that springs forth in the resurrection and life. It is summed up in the later part of this verse in just a few words, yet it is full of impact, filled with that which cannot be expressed even in a thousand words or more: "But if it dies, it bears much fruit."

DO YOU KNOW THE JOY OF "MUCH FRUIT?" THAT IS INDEED THE WHOLE ESSENCE OF A RESURRECTION LIFE FILLED WITH PLENTY.

Do you know the joy of "much fruit?" That is indeed the whole essence of a resurrection life filled with plenty. The emphasis is not just in bearing fruit, but "much" fruit—a fully producing life for yourself and others, bearing plenty and much! Being "Sent . . . " and submitting and obedient always brings "much fruit!"

SENT...

In the resurrection of Christ, Scripture distinctly states in Romans 8:29: "He would be the *firstborn* among many *brothers and sisters*." How many brethren? A whole world full of them! This is what Jesus had in His eternal mind. He saw far ahead and wide enough to include you and me. How far can we see and trust when it comes to lifting our eyes beyond the expectations of others?

Our life so dies together with Christ that in a very real way, we lose our own so-called identity. Again, it is much like Paul expressed in Galatians 2:20:

> *I have been crucified with Christ; and it is no longer I who live, but Christ lives in me; and the life which I now live in the flesh I live by faith in the Son of God, who loved me and gave Himself up for me.*

It boils down to the fact that we actually did not even choose Christ; we don't belong to ourselves, let alone to anyone else but Christ. As John 15:16 states

> *"You did not choose Me but I chose you, and appointed you that you would go and bear fruit, and that your fruit would remain, so that whatever you ask of the Father in My name He may give to you."*

This is the resurrection and chosen power working and producing according to His good will and purpose in our lives! This brings lasting results in what we do—nothing is wasted and much is gained.

Jesus does remind us that there are other standards, numerous possibilities, and other ways—but are they right? In John 8:15-16 (NIV), Jesus says, "You judge by human standards; I pass judgment on no one. But if I do judge, my decisions are true, because I am not alone. I stand with the Father, who sent me."

WHOM DO YOU STAND WITH? WHAT HUMAN STANDARDS ARE CALCULATED INTO YOUR EQUATION?

Whom do you stand with? What human standards are calculated into your equation? I know, we can find all kinds of rational excuses to place ourselves along the path of reason from the pressures of circumstances and other people. But when all is said and done—was the purpose of Christ finished? That is a solemn and heart-searching question we all need to face and cannot afford to ignore.

The context of John 8:13-18 (NIV) is tied into this exact value as the Pharisees once again challenge Jesus on this very issue:

The Pharisees challenged him, "Here you are, appearing as your own witness; your testimony is not valid." Jesus answered, "Even if I testify on my own behalf, my testimony is valid, for I know where I came from and where I am going. But you have no idea where I come from or where I am going. You judge by human standards; I pass judgment on no one. But if I do judge, my decisions are true, because I am not alone. I stand with the Father, who sent me. I am one who testifies for myself; my other witness is the Father, who sent me."

What witness do you and I have? Who chose us? Whom do we belong to? Who sent us? Here's the answer: "As my Father hath sent me, even so send I you" (John 20:21, KJV).

Let's go back to the questions at hand. Whose promotional package are we unloading? Are we hearing from heaven? What is

SENT...

the message? What is the motivation? How much are we bowing to the expectation of circumstances and opinions of others?

In all honesty, we face these questions every day. Sometimes it's very obvious; other times it is more subtle and elusive. What about personal decisions that come up during the day—do we include Christ in the equation? Educational psychologist and decision researcher Richard Feenstra has claimed there are thousands of decisions we make even during a single day:

> *Several Internet sources claim that people make 35,000 decisions a day. If we consider six hours for sleep, that is 1,944 decisions an hour. I think that 35,000 must be using a very loose definition of what it means to make a decision. Anyway, this number is very popular and all over the Internet, but to date I have not been able to locate the original research backing up that article, yet this number is repeatedly quoted. If you are able to ever find that research, let me know.*
>
> *One of the challenges is that what is or is not a decision is subjective as would be the type of decision. What is a simple decision for one person is a complex decision for another. A serious decision for one person is not serious for someone else.*[7]

Additionally, Travis Bradberry, co-author of *Emotional Intelligence 2.0*, claims:

> *A recent study from Columbia University found that we're bogged down by more than seventy decisions a day. The sheer number of decisions we have to make each day*

---

[7] "How Many Decisions does a Person Make in an Average Day?" Quora, accessed February 28, 2019, https://www.quora.com/How-many-decisions-does-a-person-make-in-an-average-day.

leads to a phenomenon called decision fatigue, whereby your brain actually tires like a muscle.[8]

A new study from the University of Texas shows that even when our brains aren't tired, they can make it very difficult for us to make good decisions. When making a decision, instead of referencing the knowledge we've accumulated, our brains focus on specific, detailed memories.

For example, if you're buying a new car and trying to decide if you should go for the leather seats, even though you know you can't afford it, your brain might focus on memories of the wonderful smell and feel of the leather seats in your brother's sports car, when it should be focused on the misery you're going to experience when making your monthly car payments. Since you don't have memories of this yet, it's a hard thing for your brain to contemplate.

Our days are filled with a constant stream of decisions. Most are mundane, but some are so important that they can haunt you for the rest of your life.[9]

I FULLY UNDERSTAND AND DO NOT EXPECT US TO BECOME SOME KIND OF "SPIRITUAL ZOMBIE" WALKING AROUND ALL DAY IN A DIVINE CLOUD OF DAZE NOT DARING TO MAKE A MOVE UNLESS THEY HEAR FROM HEAVEN.

---

8 S. S. Iyengar and M. R. Lepper, "When Choice is Demotivating: Can One Desire Too Much of a Good Thing?" *Journal of Personality and Social Psychology*, 79, no. 6 (Winter 2000): 995, https://doi.org/10.1037//0022-3514.79.6.995.

9 Michael L. Mack, Alison R. Preston, and Bradley C. Love, "Decoding the Brain's Algorithm for Categorization from Its Neural Implementation," *Current* Biology, 23, no. 10 (Fall 2013): 2023-2027, https://www.cell.com/current-biology/fulltext/S0960-9822(13)01041-5.

SENT...

Now, I fully understand and do not expect us to become some kind of "spiritual zombie" walking around all day in a divine cloud of daze not daring to make a move unless they hear from heaven. Of course, I have met people who try to portray this kind of stance, and it usually leads to a lot of confusion. I am not talking about this at all. I am talking about having a built-in God consciousness and awareness that is consciously or subconsciously sensitive to the inner promptings of the Spirit of God within us. God gave us a brain and it is there for us to use—so use it. The brain is a marvelous creation. It is the command center for the human nervous system which is a complex integrated information processing organism. God created mankind with a brain for well-being and benefit. Yet there are numerous occasions where the brain and human recourses are unmistakably limited when considering the whole picture of God, His eternity, infinity, and creation.

As much as man has done and the absolute ingenious wonders he has accomplished, he still has not come close to catching up with God, nor could he in any way even compare to the God of this universe. Yet, God in all His deity and holy eternal existence created man and woman and loved them enough, even in the middle of all their failures, to redeem them and buy them back with His own Son's death. But because this was not enough, by His grace and redemption, He then qualified man by lifting him to the justified level of where He would dwell within man and make him a temple of His holy presence!

Jesus made it very clear when He expressed in John 14:18-20:
"I will not leave you as orphans; I am coming to you.
After a little while, the world no longer is going to see Me,

but you are going to see Me; because I live, you also will live. In that day you will know that I am in My Father, and you are in Me, and I in you."

This is why Paul expressed in 1 Corinthians 6:19-20:

Or do you not know that your body is a temple of the Holy Spirit within you, whom you have from God, and that you are not your own? For you have been bought with a price: therefore glorify God in your body.

When we realize Whom we belong to, Who it is that indwells us, and Who commissions and sends us, then it is fully understandable why we would be conscious of His will and purpose in the decisions which control our daily lives. Who has more right than Christ in the purposes and direction of our lives? Who merits approval over our lives in following Christ?

Here is yet another example of the kind of pressure that was being applied to Jesus and the motivation behind the fear of reprisal and being accepted by others:

Nevertheless many, even of the rulers, believed in Him, but because of the Pharisees they were not confessing Him, so that they would not be excommunicated from the synagogue; for they loved the approval of people rather than the approval of God. —John 12:42-43

At this point, Jesus gets very emotional about this kind of pressure that the Pharisees were not only putting on Him, but on those who believed and yet became afraid. Here, the scriptures even say that Jesus cried out—there is no doubt He was raising His voice, filled with passion and emotion: "The one who believes in Me, does not believe *only* in Me but *also* in Him who sent Me. And the one who sees Me sees *Him* who sent Me." (John 12:44-45).

SENT...

Those are powerful words! What Jesus is saying here is becoming pretty clear. Then just a few verses later, Jesus emphasizes, "For I did not speak on My own, but the Father Himself who sent Me has given Me a commandment as to what to say and what to speak" (John 12:49).

He makes it resoundingly obvious and evident showing He was not going to bow down to any pressure or suggestion, nor wait for the approval of men; rather, He was on a mission with a message that was founded solely in the will, purpose, and commission of the Father, under whose authority He was sent.

So, the questions repeatedly address the titles and subtitles of this chapter. Only you can answer them. "Whose Promotional Package Are You Unloading?" Are you "Hearing from Heaven?" "What is the Message?" you are carrying? "What is the Motivation?" and to what extent are you actually "Bowing to the Expectation of Others?"

> **SO ONCE AGAIN, TO SAVE US A LOT OF WASTED TIME, ENDLESS EFFORT, DISAPPOINTMENTS, AND CONFUSION, LEADING US TOWARD AN UNHAPPY OR DISSATISFYING LIFE, IT MIGHT BE WORTH IT FOR US TO SERIOUSLY EVALUATE EVERYTHING THAT HAS BEEN SAID.**

John 5:20-24 sums up a lot of what has been said. Many of the truths we have discussed in this chapter are a resounding echo of Christ's words. They pierce the depth of the truths of the questions we have closely examined and studied thus far.

Whose Promotional Package Are You Unloading?

"For the Father loves the Son and shows Him all things that He Himself is doing; and the Father will show Him greater works than these, so that you will be amazed. For just as the Father raises the dead and gives them life, even so the Son also gives life to whom He wishes. For not even the Father judges anyone, but He has given all judgment to the Son, so that all will honor the Son even as they honor the Father. The one who does not honor the Son does not honor the Father who sent Him. "Truly, truly, I say to you, the one who hears My word, and believes Him who sent Me, has eternal life, and does not come into judgment, but has passed out of death into life."

So once again, to save us a lot of wasted time, endless effort, disappointments, and confusion, leading us toward an unhappy or dissatisfying life, it might be worth it for us to seriously evaluate everything that has been said.

"Whose Promotional Package Are You Unloading?"

CHAPTER 6

EXCLUSIVE RIGHTS

WHERE YOU FIT IN THE BIG PICTURE

In this final chapter, we arrive at what is the most important question for you and me: *Where does this leave me in the whole picture?* I think you get the picture at this point. Many questions have already been asked and challenges presented that have caused us to think about ourselves in relation to the entire subject. After all, from the very beginning of the book, we were made aware of the statement which Jesus made that established the theme of this book: "So Jesus said to them again, 'Peace be with you; as the Father has sent Me, I also send you'" (John 20:21).

Or as we saw in the ERV, "Then Jesus said again, 'Peace be with you. It was the Father who sent me, and I am now sending you in the same way.'"

SENT...

Jesus draws this parallel between His being sent by the Father and Him sending us. That is what directly ties and bonds us with this extraordinary commission.

Though we have this unusual statement, the same truths are found all throughout the Gospel of John and the entire Scripture. Yet perhaps it might be good to look at some of these other portions of scripture, along with those found in the Gospel of John where our primary focus has been. This would only reinforce the principle of Christ's direct relationship to you and me. In order to fulfill this parallel relationship—Christ to His Father and us to Christ—we have to carefully look at what the life of Christ in His relationship to His Father looked like. We have done this extensively, and it has given us a firm foundation that we can stand on to conclude this book. The context of this chapter is our relationship to Christ. He unmistakably includes us. When we interpret these verses within the full context of Scripture, it is hard to believe otherwise. But let's look at it again, as it directly relates to you and me.

I labeled this chapter "Exclusive Rights" so that we keep Christ's statements in mind. They are part of the divine purpose of God. After all, it is He who took the initiative to include us in the first place. He was the One who extended the exclusive rights to us. We could not demand them, we could not pay for them, nor could we offer anything in return. In fact, those rights were His will and purpose for our lives before we even existed. Romans 8:28-30 (AMP) says:

> *And we know [with great confidence] that God [who is deeply concerned about us] causes all things to work together [as a plan] for good for those who love God,*

to those who are called according to His plan and purpose. For those whom He foreknew [and loved and chose beforehand], He also predestined to be conformed to the image of His Son [and ultimately share in His complete sanctification], so that He would be the firstborn [the most beloved and honored] among many believers. And those whom He predestined, He also called; and those whom He called, He also justified [declared free of the guilt of sin]; and those whom He justified, He also glorified [raising them to a heavenly dignity].

Look at the words in that passage. Don't even think for a moment He did not take the incentive to include you and me! It's pretty obvious—pretty inclusive! Wow!

But let's look at what Jesus said about how we fit into the bigger picture:

"No longer do I call you slaves, for the slave does not know what his master is doing; but I have called you friends, because all things that I have heard from My Father I have made known to you." —John 15:15

And John 17:8 (AMP) says:

"For the words which You gave Me I have given them; and they received and accepted them and truly understood [with confident assurance] that I came from You [from Your presence], and they believed [without any doubt] that You sent Me."

Not only does He send us in like manner as the Father sent Him, but here in both of these verses, Christ tells us that "all things that I have heard from My Father I have made known to you" and the "words" that He had received from the Father, He now

SENT...

gives to us! What He states in the latter verse is the basis of our faith and belief in Him having been sent of the Father. Absolutely astounding! What revelation!

But there were those who would not be so quick to respond with faith and, as a result, would be left out: "The one who does not love Me does not follow My words; and the word which you hear is not Mine, but the Father's who sent Me" (John 14:24).

The connection is genuine, it is strong, and it means everything. John 13:20 tells us, "Truly, truly I say to you, the one who receives *anyone I send receives Me*; and the one who *receives Me receives Him who sent Me.*"

When Christ "Sent . . ." us, it is as if Christ Himself was being represented! It is clear as it can be here: "Anyone I send receives Me." That is powerful! But it does not stop there. Not only do those of us who are sent receive Christ, but when we receive Christ, we receive the Father Himself! Can we even begin to understand the power of "being sent"! He stands solely behind the commission of us being sent by Him.

HE STANDS SOLELY BEHIND THE COMMISSION OF US BEING SENT BY HIM.

These are the exclusive rights we write about in this chapter. This is where we fit into the whole scheme of things.

> *"Do you not believe that I am in the Father, and the Father is in Me? The words that I say to you I do not speak on My own, but the Father, as He remains in Me, does His works. Believe Me that I am in the Father and the Father is in Me; otherwise believe because of the*

works themselves. Truly, truly I say to you, the one who believes in Me, the works that I do, he will do also; and greater works than these he will do; because I am going to the Father. And whatever you ask in My name, this I will do, so that the Father may be glorified in the Son. If you ask Me anything in My name, I will do it. If you love Me, you will keep My commandments.

"I will ask the Father, and He will give you another Helper, that He may be with you forever; The Helper is the Spirit of truth, whom the world cannot receive, because it does not see Him or know Him, but you know Him because He remains with you and will be in you.

"I will not leave you as orphans; I am coming to you. After a little while, the world no longer is going to see Me, but you are going to see Me; because I live, you also will live. On that day you will know that I am in My Father, and you are in Me, and I in you." — John 14:10-20

Earlier, I drew your attention to this incredible last verse. We are in a very special position—uniquely tied into a relationship with Christ and thus to the Father—Christ in the Father, we in Christ, and Christ in us. If Jesus was in the Father and we are in Christ, then we are in the Father.

We must understand and make note of the fact that Jesus fortifies His position in the Father and then immediately turns His attention to "he who believes in Me" and moves us on to even "greater works." Who is the "he" if it is not you and me? This exclusively is it—you and I who believe!

These statements are not by accident, nor are they mere passing words. They fall into the whole category of the exclusive rights

SENT...

through the relationship which Christ has brought us into with Himself, and now on this basis, He sends us forth. He continues to promote this same principle which He Himself has been operating out of His relationship with the Father. It is not one isolated statement of fact, but it is a scriptural staple He emphasizes over and over again.

Look at what He says in John 15:4-9:

"Remain in Me, and I in you. As the branch cannot bear fruit of itself but must remain in the vine, so neither can you unless you remain in Me. I am the vine, you are the branches; the one who remains in Me, and I in him bears much fruit, for apart from Me you can do nothing. If anyone does not remain in Me, he is thrown away like a branch and dries up; and they gather them, and throw them into the fire and they are burned. If you remain in Me, and My words remain in you, ask whatever you wish, and it will be done for you. My Father is glorified by this, that you bear much fruit, and so prove to be My disciples. Just as the Father has loved Me, I also have loved you; remain in My love."

Is this not what He says again just a few verses later?

"You have not chosen Me, but I have chosen you and I have appointed and placed and purposefully planted you, so that you would go and bear fruit and keep on bearing, and that your fruit will remain and be lasting, so that whatever you ask of the Father in My name [as My representative] He may give to you." —John 15:16

In other words, it is not only us—but us together with Him! He is the vine, we are the branches. He says: "As the branch cannot bear fruit of itself." We can produce nothing without Him: "Neither *can* you unless you abide in Me." It is all part of the process of bearing fruit, even "much fruit!"

WE CANNOT BEAR MUCH FRUIT OURSELVES— OUR LIVES ARE FROM HIM AND THROUGH HIM!

But we cannot do it ourselves—our lives are from Him and through Him! He says: "Apart from Me you can do nothing." Is this not what He said of Himself in relation to the Father? I have said it before but it bears repeating, particularly here. For example, in John 5:19: "I say to you, the Son can do nothing of Himself, unless *it is* something He sees the Father doing; for whatever the Father does, these things the Son also does in the same way." Then, in verse 30, Jesus adds, "*I can do nothing on My own.* As I hear, I judge; and My judgment is righteous, because *I do not seek My own will but the will of Him who sent Me.*"

Then in verse 36, "For the works which the *Father has given me to accomplish*—the very works that I do—*testify about Me, that the Father has sent Me.*" Then on again in John 8:28-29, He expounds, "*I do nothing on My own*, but I say these things as the Father instructed Me. And He who sent Me is with Me; He has not left Me alone, *for I always do the things that are pleasing to Him.*"

So, what Jesus is telling us concerning our own strength and ability in doing what pleases Christ He Himself experienced with the Father.

This was so the Holy Spirit—the Spirit speaking Himself: "But when He, the Spirit of truth, comes, He will guide you into all the truth; for He will not speak on His own, but whatever

SENT...

He hears, He will speak; and He will disclose to you what is to come" (John 16:13).

We have the source of the Spirit of truth who will disclose and reveal to us the Spirit of revelation and truth. It all is of the Spirit of God—our connection to the vine with we as the branches, the Spirit of God within us! What a connection! What a flow of His Spirit!

> *Now on the last day, the great day of the feast, Jesus stood and cried out, saying, "If anyone is thirsty, let him come to Me and drink. The one who believes in Me, as the Scripture said, 'From his innermost being will flow rivers of living water.'" But this He said in reference to the Spirit, whom those who believed in Him were to receive; for the Spirit was not yet given, because Jesus was not yet glorified. —John 7:37-39*

John 14:26 says, "But the Helper, the Holy Spirit, whom the Father will send in My name, He will *teach you all things, and bring to your remembrance all that I said to you*." That is why John later describes this immensely powerful Holy Spirit source within us exactly how Jesus described it earlier in 1 John 2:26-28:

> *These things I have written to you concerning those who are trying to deceive you. And as for you, the anointing which you received from Him remains in you, and you have no need for anyone to teach you; but as His anointing teaches you about all things, and is true and is not a lie, and just as it has taught you, you remain in Him. Now, little children, remain in Him, so that when He appears, we may have confidence and not draw back from Him in shame at His coming.*

WE FIT DIRECTLY INTO THE MIDDLE OF THE FLOW OF HIS ANOINTING, KNOWLEDGE, AND REVELATION! WHAT A LEGACY WE ARE BORN INTO BY HIS SPIRIT!

What a connection! We fit directly into the middle of the flow of His anointing, knowledge, and revelation! What a legacy we are born into by His Spirit!

WHAT LEGACY ARE YOU LEFT WITH TO PASS ON?

Jesus passed on to us a legacy of astounding proportions! Nothing could be without Him and there is nothing we could possibly carry on by our own efforts. It would involve our free will, sacrifice, and service coupled with much work—but none of it by ourselves. With all that He requires, He is there to supply.

Christ, by the work of the cross, brings us into a union with God which no man could have even begun to imagine, not by the furthest stretch of the human mind and imagination. John 17:21 says, "That they may all be one; just as You, Father, *are* in Me and I in You, that *they also may be in Us*, so that the world may believe *that You sent Me.*"

Concluding with the foundational truth of being sent of the Father, Jesus now includes us into this unbelievable union which He had with the Father. He so absolutely and categorically includes us! This, then, is grounds for the world to believe that Christ was sent of the Father. We have now become part of the testimony of Christ—His union to the Father by not only our union to Christ, but to the Father. What is the evidence of this? It is none other than what Jesus commissioned and sent us to achieve.

SENT...

Before I move on explaining what all this entails, let me for a moment reinforce this incredible union which exists in our amazing connection to the Father through Christ!

In John 14:1-2, Jesus reveals something astounding: "Do not let your heart be troubled; believe in God, believe also in Me. In My Father's house are many rooms; *if that* were not so, I would have told you; because I am going *there* to prepare a place for you."

Here Jesus is comforting His followers, telling them not to worry and to believe in God. He also tells them to believe in Him. Then He says something very specific: "In My Father's house are many rooms...." Do you really think God has a house? Just think about it—it's God! Why would God need a house? And, would God live in a house?

I believe Jesus is speaking figuratively, much like He did when He spoke of Himself as bread in John 6:35: "Jesus said to them, 'I am the *bread* of life; the one who comes to Me will not be hungry, and the one who believes in Me will never be thirsty.'"

In fact, in this same chapter, Jesus refers to Himself in this manner at least fourteen times.

He also speaks figuratively of giving "living water," of which the lady at the well still did not understand and thought Jesus was referring to some type of literal, physical water. John 6:13-15 says:

> *Jesus answered and said to her, "Everyone who drinks of this water will thirst again; but whoever drinks of the water that I will give him shall never thirst; but the water that I will give him will become in him a well of water springing up to eternal life." The woman said to Him, "Sir, give me this water, so I will not be thirsty nor come all the way here to draw."*

In Revelation, the last book of the Bible, there is repeated figurative language in relation to Christ and the tree of life: "The leaves of the tree were for the healing of the nations" (22:2), and "a river of the water of life, clear as crystal, coming from the throne of God and of the Lamb, in the middle of its street" (22:1). This is all in symbolic figurative language filled with the depth of truth and revelation.

In like manner in John 14, I believe Christ speaks of greater things than buildings, houses, rooms, and places of physical nature either on earth or even in heaven. But in concurrence with the context of the entire chapter, it is not difficult to understand how deeply it embodies the whole concept of unity, connectedness, and being bonded and merged together. In this chapter and in later verses of chapters 12 and 13, the theme of Christ's union with the Father continues and gradually incorporates us into this same union:

> *Therefore when he had left, Jesus said, "Now is the Son of Man glorified, and God is glorified in Him; if God is glorified in Him, God will also glorify Him in Himself, and will glorify Him immediately. Little children, I am still with you a little longer. You will look for Me; and just as I said to the Jews, now I also say to you, 'Where I am going, you cannot come.' I am giving you a new commandment, that you love one another, just as I have loved you, that you also love one another. By this all men will know that you are My disciples, that you also love one another." —John 13:31-34*

SENT...

Peter doesn't get it and in his earthly way of thinking, he doesn't understand the spiritual unity Christ is speaking of, so he blurts out, "Lord, where are You going?" (John 13:36)

I may have well done the same! In the same verse, Jesus responds: "Where I am going, you cannot follow Me now; but you will follow later."

Pay special attention to "but you will follow later."

Jesus is leading him toward the union that would bring us into the spiritual bond and relationship He was about to create by His death, burial, and resurrection. Of course, in his human thinking, Peter still did not fully understand this, so he asked quite boldly: "Lord, why can I not follow You right now? I will lay down my life for You" (John 13:37).

I think Peter had things completely turned around backwards. Who was laying down their life for whom?

"Will you lay down your life for Me?" Jesus asked (v. 38). In a prophetic note, Jesus exposes Peter's human frailty and how briefly this earthly thinking would last: "Truly, truly I say to you, a rooster will not crow until you deny Me three times."

And then comes chapter 14, with the superlative, powerful comfort and preeminent, lofty union that was to occur. This is where Peter would then "follow later"! This was a whole other dimension of things related to bonding, unity, and union, the kind Jesus had with the Father and would now include Peter and the rest of us.

John 15:5 then describes it in the famous words of Christ: "I am the vine, you are the branches."

"I AM THE VINE, YOU ARE THE BRANCHES." THIS IS THE HEART OF OUR UNION WITH HIM.

This is the heart of our union with Him. So many have reduced the whole plan of salvation to merely escaping hell and getting to heaven. These are the results, not the goal or aim of our salvation. The aim of salvation is to be brought into union with Christ, and therefore the God of this universe Who created us! It is all about being together with God! We see in 2 Corinthians 5:19: "Namely, that God was in Christ *reconciling the world to Himself*, not counting their wrongdoings against them, and He has committed to us the word of reconciliation."

Let's go back to John 16:

"He will glorify Me, for He will take of Mine and will disclose it to you. All things that the Father has are Mine; therefore I said that He takes of Mine and will disclose it to you." —vv. 14-15

"In that day you will ask in My name, and I do not say to you that I will request of the Father on your behalf; for the Father Himself loves you, because you have loved Me and have believed that I came forth from the Father. —vv. 26-27

John 17:3 says, "And this is eternal life, that *they may know You*, the only true God, and Jesus Christ whom *You have sent*." Reading further, Jesus tells us:

"I have revealed Your name to the men whom You gave Me out of the world; they were Yours and You gave them to Me, and they have followed Your word. Now **they** *have come to know that everything You have given Me is from*

SENT...

You; for the words which You gave Me I have given to them; and they received them and truly understood that I came forth from You, and they believed that You sent Me. I ask on their behalf; I do not ask on behalf of the world, but on the behalf of those whom You have given Me; because they are Yours; and all things that are Mine are Yours, and Yours are Mine; and I have been glorified in them." —John 17:6-10

This is the fantastic legacy, a perfect union with Christ! We are left with this message to pass on to the world as good news of where we really belong in the big picture of things and what our purpose is here on earth being send of Christ!

He continues in verse 26, "And I have made *Your name known to them*, and will make it known, so that the *love with which You loved Me may be in them, and I in them.*"

There is the theme that runs so distinctly through chapters 12-17. This is why the scripture in John 14, right in the middle of all of this, talks about relationship, not a house. It is all about who you are in Him and He in you and Jesus in His Father and us in Him.

This should help us better understand that we have an "abode" or place with the Father if we understand it all in the full context of the scriptures that surround this passage. Let's just follow through with this thought again in the context of where it is written. He said He was going to prepare us a place "as an abode with the Father" (author paraphrase). Continue to bear with me for a bit longer, so I can bring this all into proper perspective.

You see Jesus goes on to explain in John 14:3-4, "If I go and prepare a place for you, I will come again and *receive you to Myself*, that *where I am, there you may be also.* And you know the way where I am going."

Thomas questions Him in verse 5 much the same way Peter questioned Christ: "Lord, we do not know where You are going, how do we know the way?" Jesus then makes the well-known reply in verse 6, "*I am the way, and the truth, and the life*; no one *comes to the Father except through Me.*"

This is the key, very clear and concise. Like I have said earlier, He was not talking about places or objects; He was not even suggesting they take some specific route. He talks about a person: "I am the way, and the truth, and the life." In other words: "I am" is what you are looking for: "I am all of it—that's it!" You don't even get near the Father unless you first go through Christ! It's all about relationship, His relationship to the Father and the Father to Him. That is why I have taken the time to clearly indicate the context of the chapters around this verse. The message is all about "abiding" and "being"—about relationships. That is why Jesus says that no one can ever come to the Father except through Him. It was not coming to a house in heaven that Jesus is talking about. He is talking about coming into the very presence of the Father—God Himself!

> **IT WAS NOT COMING TO A HOUSE IN HEAVEN THAT JESUS IS TALKING ABOUT. HE IS TALKING ABOUT COMING INTO THE VERY PRESENCE OF THE FATHER—GOD HIMSELF!**

Philip also challenges Jesus in verse 8: "Lord, *show us the Father*, and it is enough for us."

SENT...

Philip's challenge leads us directly to a series of answers in which Jesus shows us the powerful union He had with the Father: "Jesus said to him, 'Have I been with you for so long a time, and *yet you have not come to know Me*, Philip? The one who has *seen Me has seen the Father*; how *can* you say, 'Show us the Father?'" (v. 8)

At this point a powerful discourse follows, where Jesus shows them the Father and tells them where His abode really is!

> *"Do you not believe that I am in the Father, and the Father is in Me? The words that I say to you I do not speak on My own, but the Father, as He remains in Me, does His works. Believe Me that I am in the Father and the Father is in Me; otherwise believe because of the works themselves. "—vv. 10-11*

Where was Jesus? He was "in the Father" and the Father in Him! That is why He said at the beginning of the chapter in verse 3, "And if I go and prepare *a place for you*, I am coming again and *will take you to Myself,* so that *where I am, there you also will be.*"

In other words, He was saying, "I have my abode with the Father and you will also." Take specific notice of the fact that Jesus says: "Where I am, there you may be also." "Where I am," not where I will be. He was speaking of His place in the Father. The fact becomes inclusive—that we might be there also! These are our "exclusive rights!" This "exclusive right"—bought and given to us freely by Christ! That is the whole plan of redemption, man being redeemed to God Himself by way of the person of Christ! The book of John is full of this! This was bringing man into fellowship with the God of this universe through the redeeming Christ and His sacrifice.

Notice also just before He said this, Jesus also said: "I will receive you to Myself." This is exactly what He said earlier in John 12:32-33: "And I, if I am lifted up from the earth, *will draw all people to Myself.*" Now He was saying this to indicate what *kind of death* He was going to die.

Through the cross we have been taken into Christ! This is what Romans 6 is all about:

> *Or do you not know that all of us who have been baptized into Christ Jesus have been baptized into His death? Therefore we have been buried with Him through baptism into death, so that, just as Christ was raised from the dead through the glory of the Father, so we too might walk in newness of life. For if we have become united with Him in the likeness of His death, certainly we shall also be in the likeness of His resurrection, knowing this, that our old self was crucified with Him, in order that our body of sin might be done away with, so that we would no longer be slaves to sin; for the one who has died is freed from sin. Now if we have died with Christ, we believe that we shall also live with Him, knowing that Christ, having been raised from the dead, is never to die again; death no longer is master over Him. For the death that He died, He died to sin once for all time; but the life that He lives, He lives to God. So you too, consider yourselves to be dead to sin, but alive to God in Christ Jesus.*

What a powerful portion of scripture and revelation, showing us the power of His death, burial, and resurrection in us! It is not just the fact we are forgiven of our sins as a matter of heaven or hell, but here is the entire wonderful truth brought forth so

SENT...

powerfully showing that, indeed, we are united with Christ through His death, burial, and resurrection! That is our life together with Him, right here and now—today!

Now back to John 14:3, "I will receive you to Myself." By the work of the cross, we are in Him. Now, in the same context in verse 10, Jesus says "I am in the Father, and the Father is in Me." He then presents one of the most powerful scriptures in the Bible that links us to the very center and being of God Himself! He says, "In that day you will know that I am in My Father, and you in Me, and I in you" (v. 11).

> **IF JESUS IS IN THE FATHER, AND WE ARE IN JESUS, AND JESUS IS IN US, THEN WE ARE ALSO IN THE FATHER!**

If Jesus is in the Father, and we are in Jesus, and Jesus is in us, then we are also in the Father! We are joined to the God of this universe, we are one with Him! This is the core of redemption!

I studied something in geometry during high school called "Axiom 1," created by a gentleman Euclid of Alexandria, a Greek mathematician, who was often referred to as the "founder of geometry" or the "father of geometry." He was active in Alexandria during the reign of Ptolemy I (323–283 BC). Yet his axiom continue to be used even to this day. The definition of an axiom is "a rule or a statement that is accepted as true without proof. An axiom is also called a postulate." [10] To postulate is to "suggest or

---

10 "What is an Axiom?" Quora, Accessed June 18, 2019, https://www.quora.com/What-is-Axiom.

assume the existence, fact, or truth of (something) as a basis for reasoning, discussion, or belief."[11]

Euclid's Axiom: "Things which are equal to the same thing are also equal to one another."[12]

Therefore, an axiom does not need proof. It is completely logical—there can be no other conclusion. We can, in a sense, apply Euclid's axiom to this Scripture: "In that day you will know that I am in My Father, and you in Me, and I in you" (v. 11).

If Jesus is in the Father, and we are in Jesus, and He in us, then we can assume that we are in the Father.

Totally complete! Totally connected!

Paul really got a hold of this magnificent truth throughout his revelations and writings, as he so clearly points out in 2 Corinthians 5:18-20:

> *Now all these things are from God, who reconciled us to Himself through Christ and gave us the ministry of reconciliation, namely, that God was in Christ reconciling the world to Himself, not counting their wrongdoings against them, and He has committed to us the word of reconciliation. Therefore, we are ambassadors for Christ, as though God were making an appeal through us; we beg you on behalf of Christ, be reconciled to God.*

Again, this is the legacy left to us, and in the "ministry of reconciliation" we pass it on! This legacy is what John 14 is all about! An entire book could be written on that chapter alone!

---

11 "Postulate, *Encyclopedia.Com*, www.encyclopedia.com/science-and-technology/mathematics/mathematics/postulate#:~:text=pos%C2%B7tu%C2%B7late%20%E2%80%A2%20v,environmentalists%20 might%20have%20a%20case.

12 "Euclid," *Wikipedia*, https://en.wikipedia.org/wiki/Euclid.

SENT...

What is so outstanding in all of this is the fact that Jesus was so tied to the Father by birth, by Spirit, and by divine will and purpose! Jesus makes these statements over and over, especially in the book of John and even numerous passages throughout the Gospels. There are many prophetic words throughout the New Testament and even the Old Testament, depicting this very unity and bond, such as Isaiah's prophetic words of the birth of Christ (Isaiah 9:6): "For a Child will be born to us, a Son will be given to us; And the government will rest on His shoulders; And *His name* will be called Wonderful Counselor, *Mighty God, Eternal Father,* Prince of Peace."

So, this union was precisely prophesied and his titles were made known long before His coming.

Now again, note what Jesus says here in John 14:16-17:

"I will ask the Father, and He will give you another Helper, that He may be with you forever; the Helper is the Spirit of truth, whom the world cannot receive, because it does not see Him or know Him, but you know Him because He remains with you and will be in you."

And then He continues in John 14:26, "But the Helper, the Holy Spirit, whom the Father will send in My name, He will teach you all things, and remind you of all that I said to you."

Without a doubt, we see that it is the Father who "gives" and "sends" through the Holy Spirit He is speaking of in this passage. What is interesting is the fact that Jesus says, "He remains with you and will be in you."

Remember the outstanding statement Jesus makes that confirms what we see in verse 26: "In that day you will know that I am in My Father, and you in Me, and *I in you*" (v. 20).

Here, Jesus states that He is in us—"I in you." Before this, He states the Spirit of truth "will be in you."

Are you seeing the connections? Now, look further. Jesus says in verse 18, "I will not leave you as orphans; *I will come to you*." He saying He will come to us. Who then, is finally coming? Is there a misunderstanding? No, not for a moment. He is the One and same Spirit that is coming. Jesus is in the Father and the Father is in Him—One and the same Holy Spirit—the Spirit of God!

> **HE IS THE ONE AND SAME SPIRIT THAT IS COMING. JESUS IS IN THE FATHER AND THE FATHER IS IN HIM—ONE AND THE SAME HOLY SPIRIT—THE SPIRIT OF GOD!**

It is no different when we look at the birth of Christ in Matthew 1:18-20.

> *Now the birth of Jesus the Messiah was as follows: when His mother Mary had been betrothed to Joseph, before they came together she was found to be pregnant by the Holy Spirit. And her husband Joseph, since he was a righteous man and did not want to disgrace her, planned to send her away secretly. But when he had thought this over, behold, an angel of the Lord appeared to him in a dream, saying, "Joseph, son of David, do not be afraid to take Mary as your wife; for the Child who has been conceived in her is of the Holy Spirit."*

Who, then, was the father of Jesus? Was it the Holy Spirit or was it the Father? There can be no question about it, it was all the

SENT...

same Spirit—the Spirit of God. There is but one Spirit of God; there is only one God!

Jesus Himself quotes Old Testament scripture in Mark 12:29, "Jesus answered, 'The foremost is, 'Hear, O Israel! The Lord is our God, the Lord is One.'" Again, Jesus teaches about the woman of Samaria at the well, "*God is spirit*, and those who worship Him must worship in *spirit* and truth" (John 4:24).

It is by way of the Spirit of God that we are joined to God. Paul sums it up in Ephesians 4:4-6: "There is *one body and one Spirit*, just as also you were called in *one hope* of your calling; *one* Lord, *one* faith, *one* baptism, *one* God and Father of all who is over all and *through all and in all*."

John continues to describe it so well in 1 John 3:24: "The *one* who keeps His commandments *remains in Him, and He in him*. We know by this that *He remains in us*, by the *Spirit* whom He has given us."

The same truth is so clearly expounded by Paul in 1 Corinthians 8:6 "Yet for us there is *only one God, the Father*, from *whom are all things*, and *we exist for Him*; and *one Lord, Jesus Christ*, by *whom are all things*, and *we exist through Him*." Further, in 1 Corinthians 12:13, we read, "For by *one Spirit* we were all baptized into *one body*, whether Jews or Greeks, whether slaves or free, and we were all made to drink of *one Spirit*." Finally, Paul states, "But the *one* who joins himself to the *Lord is one spirit with Him*" (1 Corinthians 6:17).

There were those who would not be in this same category. Sadly, the Pharisees and chief priests in all their self-righteousness and rituals did not want to understand and were not open to this kind of union. Further back in John 7:33-36, Jesus stated:

> *"For a little while longer I am going to be with you, and then I am going to Him who sent Me. You will seek Me, and will not find Me; and where I am, you cannot come." The Jews then said to one another, "Where does this man intend to go that we will not find Him? He does not intend to go to the Dispersion among the Greeks, and teach the Greeks, does He? What is this statement that He said, 'You will seek Me, and will not find Me; and where I am, you cannot come?'"*

He repeated much of the same in the following chapter:

> *These words He spoke in the treasury, as He taught in the temple area; and no one arrested Him, because His hour had not yet come. Then He said again to them, "I am going away, and you will look for Me, and will die in your sin; where I am going, you cannot come." So the Jews were saying, "Surely He will not kill Himself, will He, since He says, 'Where I am going, you cannot come?'"* —John 8:20-22

I wonder how many are in the same frame of mind today. They have all the trappings of religion and works, yet this kind of union is far for many. Even some of the company we keep and those in our churches who are very close to us seem to believe the central issue is only to make heaven. They often believe the sooner, the better; they are primarily motivated to escape hell; but alas, they have no union or relationship. There is none of the victory and excitement of living with Him and He with them. Being sent by Him to do His will through our lives by completing the tasks set before them and fulfilling the divine potential Christ has for them is the farthest thing from their minds. They are often living lives

SENT...

of greed and selfishness and even using scripture to sing songs of owning a "mansion" in heaven, next door to Jesus; yet sadly, they miss the close bond with Christ that He has created for them and with them right now here on earth.

Jesus makes it very clear that this bond could have never existed if He had simply stayed around in physical form with His followers trailing behind Him. That is why He stated in John 16:7: "But I tell you the truth, *it is to your advantage* that I am leaving; for if I do not leave, the Helper will not come to you; *but if I go, I will send Him to you.*"

> **CHRIST SUPERSEDES THE NATURAL AND DRAWS US INTO THE SPIRITUAL, THE REALM OF HIS KINGDOM, HIS THOUGHTS, AND EXISTENCE.**

We often fall into the trap of thinking, *It would have been great to have lived in Jesus's time*, or *wouldn't it be great to have Jesus here with us in "full view."* No, as He stated, it would not have been to our advantage, which is directly at odds with our natural thinking. But Christ supersedes the natural and draws us into the spiritual, the realm of His kingdom, His thoughts, and existence. Now, it is us together with Him, He in us and we in Him, together with the eternal God of this universe and beyond! It causes my heart, mind, and soul to expand to the point of explosion because of the absolute thrill of Christ alive in me and I in Him! No matter the circumstances, no matter the earthly limitations, no matter the outward appearances, I am living out the very purposes of Christ here on earth today!

This is why He continues to add through John that we are not only connected to Christ, but by this unbelievable union, we are directly joined to the Father:

"These things I have spoken to you in figurative language; an hour is coming when I will no longer speak to you in figurative language, but will tell you plainly of the Father. In that day you will ask in My name, and I do not say to you that I will request of the Father on your behalf; for the Father Himself loves you, because you have loved Me and have believed that I came forth from the Father. I came forth from the Father and have come into the world; I am leaving the world again and going to the Father." —John 16:25-28

In John 17, we see the Jesus's prayer to the Father, which confirms much of what we have already discovered and reveals much of the legacy we are to pass on as it was passed on to Jesus from the Father; Now we must pass on the legacy we received from Jesus:

"Father, the hour has come; glorify Your Son, so that the Son may glorify You, just as You gave Him authority over all mankind, so that to all whom You have given Him, He may give eternal life. And this is eternal life, that they may know You, the only true God, and Jesus Christ whom You have sent. I glorified You on the earth, by accomplishing the work which You have given Me to do. And now You, Father, glorify Me together with Yourself, with the glory which I had with You before the world existed. —John 17:1-5

What a concluding statement of a ministry so linked to and birthed from the very purpose and will of the Father! Then,

SENT...

Jesus continues His prayer, and again includes you and me. Note it carefully:

> *"I have revealed Your name to the men whom You gave Me out of the world; they were Yours and You gave them to Me, and they have followed Your word. Now they have come to know that everything You have given Me is from You; for the words which You gave Me I have given to them; and they received them and truly understood that I came forth from You, and they believed that You sent Me.* —John 17:6-8

There are two major facts that come into focus here. First, it's all about keeping the "word" Jesus Himself received of the Father—all of what was given to Jesus of the Father. It was believing that it came from the Father. And second, the most important conclusion in this statement that consistently reoccurs is: "You sent Me."

This was the backbone statement on which Christ rested His case. Indeed, it does recur over and over in so many of the statements Christ makes, in so many of His declarations, in numerous situations and occasions, not only with His disciples, but with the religious leaders and Pharisees. This is what Christ unwaveringly stood on.

Can we say this? This is the question that has caused me to stop dead in my tracks before proceeding again. This is the question which causes me to fall before Him in all His majesty, bowing not only to His grace and love, but to His supremacy and authority. This is all so that I may stand fast to the calling and purpose of my life before Him, so that He may live His will and purpose through my life, every single day.

I have developed a habit over the years—counting every single day. As I write this, I have been on the planet for 27,780 days. In fact, I have 1,420 days left before I am eighty years old! What will I do when I am eighty? I'll keep counting!

Why do I do this? It is not only for fun or entertainment. I do this for several reasons. First of all, I value every day because it is a day that God has given me. It is a gift. My day is His day—it all belongs to Him, so it is my legacy and my destiny, given by God to me. In turn, you have your days in the same manner!

This brings me to my second point. The days He gives me are different from anyone else's. Of the 8.8 billion—and counting—people on the planet, not one of their days is like the one I have! Think of it. The day God gives me is for me and me alone! That goes for all of us. The day God gives you is uniquely yours! Think of the variety of days and the uniqueness of each person. Each of those days changes for every single person, every day. Wow! It blows my mind. It is fantastic! Each day is part of the legacy and destiny God has gifted to each one of us.

I cannot carry a single day forward. When the clock strikes midnight, that day is gone, never to be retrieved and relived. In spite of the saying that we have to "save time," we cannot do it. Time ticks on, and we can do nothing about it. So, I just have this one day to make it count. Do what I will with it, tomorrow, it is history—gone forever!

You can see how time is even more valuable than money. You can save and keep money, and if you lose it, you can make more—but you cannot do that with time. So time becomes an important part of how we use what God has given as a legacy to us. Our

SENT...

relationship with God is eternal, but how we use it here on earth becomes of utmost importance.

Does not the Bible tell us that counting is a wise thing to do? Psalm 90:12 says, "So teach us to number our days, That we may present to You a heart of wisdom." In fact, since this is the case, I go several steps further in dealing with days and time. I have a list of nineteen objectives, projects, or goals I have worked out very carefully and in deep conviction before God. I write down my life responsibilities—to care for my family and follow God's will and purpose—and the reasons why I am responsible for these. I then budget this time. I budget exactly like you would budget money.

I consider not only this but why I should limit my God-given goals and objectives to even the time I have now while living. Why not live my days for the benefit of those who come after me, passing on the legacy I have received? We all understand the idea of wills and testaments. Yet let us live out the purposes of God for the kingdom of God's sake in what Christ may have sent us to do for future generations! Jesus did this and is even today continuing His work on earth through His legacy of union with mankind to be passed on from generation to generation.

In order to do this, we need to be diligent in what He has sent us to do now and what we will pass on. How does He want us to use our time and goals to touch those who continue to live far after we have ceased to be here? I developed my own method by which to track my days, so they will extend to the end of my life and beyond. I keep track of my time—days, months, and years—evaluating very carefully my God-given time to stay on track and be accountable for what God has sent me to do.

I take this so seriously that my good friend and professional coach, John Caplin, holds me accountable each month to accomplish this. This is not only making my life effective now but even beyond my days by letting me touch the lives of others by passing on a legacy, even as you read this book, to you.

Jesus continues to expand on this principle in John 17:9-10:

"I ask on their behalf; I do not ask on behalf of the world, but on behalf of those whom You have given Me; because they are Yours; and all things that are Mine are Yours, and Yours are Mine; and I have been glorified in them."

What a statement and final conclusion—"I have been glorified in them." I wonder if we can grasp the extent of what Jesus is praying. Our legacy is not only what was passed on to Jesus but what Jesus has passed on to us. It is a product of Christ being "glorified" in us!

> **OUR LEGACY IS NOT ONLY WHAT WAS PASSED ON TO JESUS BUT WHAT JESUS HAS PASSED ON TO US. IT IS A PRODUCT OF CHRIST BEING "GLORIFIED" IN US!**

Can you grasp this? In John 17:4 Jesus prays: "I glorified You on the earth by *accomplishing the work which You have given Me to do.*" Christ glorified the Father by accomplishing the work the Father gave Him to do. Now we glorify Christ in the work Jesus has given us to do! What a legacy for us to pass this on to the world today! What is that worth to us?! It is so complete, so absolute and final! What a commission and purpose to be sent by Christ.

SENT...

Christ here clarifies the fact that all authority of the Father and heaven stands behind and together with Christ in His role as a "passer" of the world's work to us in His name. John 17:11 states: *"I am no longer going to be in the world; and yet they themselves are in the world, and I come to You. Holy Father, keep them in Your name, the name which You have given Me, that they may be one even as We are."*

He almost repeats the same thing again in the very next verse: *"While I was with them, I was keeping them in Your name which You have given Me; and I guarded them and not one of them perished but the son of perdition, so that the Scripture would be fulfilled." —John 17:12*

Even the one who was lost was in the sovereign eternal plan of God, so "Scripture would be fulfilled." The extent of it can hardly be understood but it is there.

Jesus said much more concerning the authority under whose Name these "exclusive rights" are passed on in John 14:26: "But the Helper, the Holy Spirit whom the Father will send in *My name*, He will *teach* you all things, and remind you of all that I said to you."

The authority is unmistakably the name of Jesus! The authority that stands with this name is that of all heaven itself, and above all—God Himself!

For this reason, it is written in Philippians 2:8-11:
And being found in appearance as a man, He humbled Himself by becoming obedient to the point of death: death on a cross. For this reason also God highly exalted Him and bestowed on Him the name which is above every name, so that at the name of Jesus every knee will bow,

of those who are in heaven and on earth and under the earth, and that every tongue will confess that Jesus Christ is Lord, to the glory of God the Father.

That is why we are instructed in Colossians 3:17, "Whatever you do in word or deed, *do everything in the name of the Lord Jesus*, giving thanks through Him to God the Father."

And so the "Exclusive Rights" are passed on from the Father to Jesus who then uses His right to pass it on to us! It is also our legacy that we are included into the rights given to Christ by His authority and His Name, as He sends us! We have the authority to use His Name—the name of Jesus! This is so fantastic! It is so humbling, it makes us desire to fall prostrate before Him and acknowledge the greatness of His being!

Christ did not only want us to recognize His supremacy and power, but He strongly encourages us to ask and act on the basis of this authority. This is exactly what Jesus is saying in John 15:16: "You did not choose Me but I chose you, and appointed you that you would go and bear fruit, and *that* your fruit would remain, *so that whatever you ask of the Father in My name He may give to you.*" And John 16:23 tells us, "And on that day you will not question Me about anything. Truly, truly I say to you, if you ask the *Father* for anything *in My name*, He will give it to you."

And so Jesus instructs us in the authority of His name:

"The one who has believed and has been baptized will be saved; but the one who has not believed will be condemned. These signs will accompany those who have believed: in My name they will cast out demons, they will speak with new tongues; they will pick up serpents, and if they drink any deadly poison, it will not harm

SENT...

them; they will lay hands on the sick, and they will recover." —Mark 16:16-18

We move into the world on the authority of His name—the name of Jesus! The apostles went forth to evangelize, proclaiming salvation in the name of Jesus: "And it shall be that everyone who calls on the name of the Lord will be saved" (Acts 2:21).

Along with the gospel being preached and the kingdom of God being proclaimed in words and miraculous signs, all New Testament recorded baptisms were associated with and performed in this name: "Peter said to them, 'Repent, and each of you be baptized in the name of Jesus Christ for the forgiveness of your sins; and you will receive the gift of the Holy Spirit'" (Acts 2:38). We see in Acts 2:41, "So then, those who had received his word were baptized; and that day there were added about three thousand souls."

The Bible also tells us that, "But when they believed Philip as he was preaching the good news about the kingdom of God and the name of Jesus Christ, both men and women were being baptized" (Acts 8:12). Skipping forward a few verses, we learn:

As they went along the road they came to some water; and the eunuch said, "Look! Water! What prevents me from being baptized?" And Philip said, "If you believe with all your heart, you may." And he answered and said, "I believe that Jesus Christ is the Son of God." And he ordered that the chariot stop; and they both went down into the water, Philip as well as the eunuch, and he baptized him. —vv. 36-38

And in Acts 19:3-6, we learn more:

And he said, "Into what then were you baptized?" And they said, "Into John's baptism." Paul said, "John baptized with a baptism of repentance, telling the people to believe in Him who was coming after him, that is, in Jesus." When they heard this, they were baptized in the name of the Lord Jesus. And when Paul had laid his hands upon them, the Holy Spirit came on them, and they began speaking with tongues and prophesying.

The powerhouse of heaven brings us revelation, knowledge, and the legacy to carry out what Christ sent and commissioned us to do, all in His name—the name of Jesus!

> **THE POWERHOUSE OF HEAVEN BRINGS US REVELATION, KNOWLEDGE, AND THE LEGACY TO CARRY OUT WHAT CHRIST SENT AND COMMISSIONED US TO DO, ALL IN HIS NAME—THE NAME OF JESUS!**

Over and over, Jesus emphasizes the "name."

Accompanied by signs, the apostles went as far as to declare in great faith and boldness:

"Let it be known to all of you and to all the people of Israel, that by the name of Jesus Christ the Nazarene, whom you crucified, whom God raised from the dead— by this name this man stands here before you in good health. He is the stone which was rejected by you, the builders, but which became the chief cornerstone. And there is salvation in no one else; for there is no other name under heaven that has been given among mankind by which we must be saved." —Acts 4:10-12

SENT...

So powerful, so exclusive, and so designed by God Almighty for the salvation of mankind!

The prayer Jesus prays to pass His legacy on to us persists so deeply today that it is hard for our human minds to comprehend. We continue to peer into it by listening to Jesus's prayer to the Father in John 17:13-19:

> *"But now I am coming to You; and these things I speak in the world so that they may have My joy made full in themselves. I have given them Your word; and the world has hated them because they are not of the world, even as I am not of the world. I am not asking You to take them out of the world, but to keep them from the evil one. They are not of the world, even as I am not of the world. Sanctify them in the truth; Your word is truth. Just as You sent Me into the world, I also sent them into the world. And for their sakes I sanctify Myself, so that they themselves also may be sanctified in truth."*

Again, this is the key theme of this book: "Peace be with you; as the Father has sent Me, I also send you" (John 20:21). Notice He makes this same remark in John 17:18, almost word-for-word: *"Just as You sent Me into the world, I also sent them into the world."*

> **WITH THIS COMMISSION WE NOT ONLY HAVE A LEGACY OF EXCLUSIVE RIGHTS BUT ALSO THE DRIVING FORCE AND POWER THAT ACCOMPANIES IT.**

It is so important to realize that with this commission we not only have a legacy of exclusive rights but also the driving force and power that accompanies it. Our attention should be drawn to the joy of Christ deposited in us. Whatever it takes, we move with this legacy of joy, in the midst of persecution and hardships, just as He did, empowered by Christ Himself. As Hebrews 12:2 says, "Looking only at Jesus, the originator and perfecter of the faith, who for the joy set before Him endured the cross, despising the shame, and has sat down at the right hand of the throne of God."

And so He passes this on to us and we carry His blessing forward even in the midst of persecution:

"Blessed are you when the people hate you, and when they exclude you, and insult you, and scorn your name as evil, on account of the Son of Man. Rejoice on that day and jump for joy, for behold, your reward is great in heaven. For their fathers used to treat the prophets the same way. But woe to you who are rich, for you are receiving your comfort in full." —Luke 6:22-24

We have an enemy who hates us—there is a war going on, yet we do not flinch, because we are under His divine orders and commands. Moreover, we are joined to Him, filled with His very purposes, will, and even joy!

Oh, how often we groan and moan wanting our circumstances to change. We want to escape it all. But Christ says, "I speak in this world." Sure, circumstances may change but they also may not. Yet, in the middle of our battle even Jesus says there is no retreat (John 17:15), "I am not asking You to take them out of the world, but to keep them from the evil one." And that He does—the devil, the evil one, Satan, cannot get us because we are kept by the Father, and on top of it all, we get to walk out in the victory of Christ! That is why we can cast out demons and hell is

SENT...

afraid of us! Remember when Jesus says, "I have given them Your word" (John 17:14).

We have the joy made full in ourselves, and then we have the "word." We have the word of the Father, as Jesus decreed, "I have given them Your word." We are well equipped with His word and His joy!

John 15:11 tells us, "These things I have spoken to you so that My joy may be in you, and that your joy may be made full." Jesus continues to speak about His joy (John 16:24): "Until now you have asked for nothing in My name; ask and you will receive, so that your joy may be made full."

A little later, he continues in His prayer in John 17:17-19 to demonstrate what we have as an extension of the Word for our lives here on earth:

"Sanctify them in the truth; Your word is truth. Just as You sent Me into the world, I also have sent them into the world. And for their sakes I sanctify Myself, so that they themselves also may be sanctified in truth."

It is the position of being sanctified! Sanctified means set apart as or declared holy; consecrated." We are not sanctified by our own rights or righteousness but the sanctified Christ living within us walking out a sanctified life in His Word and truth. We are sanctified by a powerful source of Christ Himself working within us. That is why He says in verse 19: "*And for their sakes I sanctify Myself,* that they themselves also may be sanctified in truth."

Some assume these words were only for the disciples of that time, but here He says specifically "*but also for those who believe in Me*". That is all of us who believe!

Exclusive Rights

"I am not asking on behalf of these alone, but also for those who believe in Me through their word; that they may all be one; even as You, Father, are in Me and I in You, that they also may be in Us, so that the world may believe that You sent Me." —vv. 20-21

What amazing inclusive words that tie us so completely to Christ and God Himself. With all of this, it also brings us again to "that they may also be in Us"—inclusive to the whole foundational purpose of Christ's ministry, work, and function on earth. He ends with "so that the world may believe that You sent Me"

The words "You sent Me" take on a proportion totally beyond anything expressed in the words themselves. They encompass the foundational purposes of Christ for mankind which are believing and having faith in Him: the One who is behind the sending, who decides who will be sent, and who determines who will receive those sent. That is the plan of salvation and the redemption of mankind, the kingdom of God, and its proclamation! This is birthed together with His sovereignty over this world, the world beyond, and for all space, time, and eternity! That is why Jesus so frequently emphasized this phrase, and only those who had ears to hear and a heart to understand could begin to comprehend its fullest extent. It was a revelation of deep, untold truths that had profound effects.

This is repeatedly echoed even more throughout His prayer and cannot be overlooked or ignored. It repeatedly emerges and is lived out throughout the pages of scripture, as we have closely observed in the book of John. The pattern is there, consistent, and constant. It is there in the daily life of Christ—the words which He passed on to those who listened and had a heart to hear were

SENT...

the same words that bounced off of those who refused to hear. The words were given for all and they reach us still today, years and years later—still fresh, vibrant, and living, flowing off the pages of scripture and because of that, His Spirit continues to flow through us.

Listen, listen, and listen again:

> *"The glory which You have given Me I also have given to them, that they may be one, just as We are one; I in them and You in Me, that they may be perfected in unity, so that the world may know that You sent Me, and You loved them, just as You have loved Me. Father, I desire that they also, whom You have given Me, be with Me where I am, so that they may see My glory which You have given Me, for You loved Me before the foundation of the world." —John 17:22-24*

Oh, what abounding, powerful words! What a mighty unfolding of God's revelation! Christ finishes His intimate prayer with His Father in the next two verses:

> *"O righteous Father, although the world has not known You, yet I have known You; and these have known that You sent Me; and I have made Your name known to them, and will make it known, so that the love with which You loved Me may be in them, and I in them." —vv. 25-26*

In the final phrases of this prayer, so profoundly deep and filled with revelation, Jesus once again refers back to the key phrase: "these have known that You sent Me," an all-important truth for Christ and His message—once again! Then, the fact He has made known His name and shared God's divine love in us comes from the final conclusion that He be in us! Truth, recognition, and revelation are combined together with the final conclusion of His prayer when He says, "I in them!" These words are so powerful, so full, and so complete to the whole plan of salvation.

> **TRUTH, RECOGNITION, AND REVELATION ARE COMBINED TOGETHER WITH THE FINAL CONCLUSION OF HIS PRAYER WHEN HE SAYS, "I IN THEM!"**

Our legacy is to pass these revelations on to those around us and declare them to the world! It is exactly what the disciples of Jesus were sent out to do from the beginning—for God-loving people to declare the kingdom of God to a world in need and introduce them to a relationship with Him! We find this mission in 2 Corinthians 5:17-19:

> *Therefore if anyone is in Christ, this person is a new creation; the old things passed away; behold, new things have come. Now all these things are from God, who reconciled us to Himself through Christ and gave us the ministry of reconciliation, namely, that God was in Christ reconciling the world to Himself, not counting their wrongdoings against them, and He has committed to us the word of reconciliation.*

> **I HOPE WE AS CHRISTIANS DO NOT MISS IT EITHER!**

This final scripture thoroughly summarizes the theme of this book. The world has no part in reconciliation, nor can it

SENT...

understand it unless they believe. They are missing out on the "connection" with God they so desperately need. I hope we as Christians do not miss it either!

CONCLUSION

There once was a man....

After the profound introduction of the deity of Christ in the beginning verses of the Gospel of John, it is noteworthy that the next few verses start with: "There came a man *sent* from God, whose name was John" (John 1:6).

This is the first time the word "sent" is used in the book of John. The last time it is used is in in the conclusion at the end of the book: "As the Father has *sent* Me, I also *send* you" (John 20:21).

In the span between and including these scriptures there are exactly forty-two times this one word "sent" is used in reference to Jesus having been "sent" of the Father. And the last time then comes to us in the form of His commission to us as "send"—"I also send you."

> **IT STARTS WITH A DIVINE COMMISSIONING, AND IT ENDS WITH A DIVINE COMMISSIONING—ALL BEING "SENT."**

SENT...

It starts with a divine commissioning, and it ends with a divine commissioning—all being "Sent."

First both were sent of God and both died a merciless death. Both were questioned by the religious leaders and both were denied by them, yet both had followers and many believed.

Both spoke of revelation and exalted God.

Yet there were others who were also sent but not by God. They were sent by those who did not trust or follow God but their own religious ways and self-righteousness. Their inquiry was not out of a desire or thirst for God, as we see in John 1:19-22:

> *This is the testimony of John, when the Jews sent priests and Levites to him from Jerusalem to ask him, "Who are you?" Then they said to him, "Who are you? Tell us, so that we may give an answer to those who sent us?"*

The priests and Levites from the holy city of Jerusalem were also sent but not like John, "a man sent of God," nor like Jesus, because it was the "Father who sent Him." No, the Jews, secular and religious people, came from Jerusalem, but they did not get their commission from "above" like John humbly witnessed of Jesus in John 3:30-32:

> *"He must increase, but I must decrease. He who comes from above is above all, the one who is only from the earth is of the earth and speaks of the earth. He who comes from heaven is above all. What He has seen and heard, of this He testifies; and no one accepts His testimony."*

No, they could not receive His testimony, because they were of the earth and spoke of the earth. They answered not to God but were concerned that they may give an answer to those who sent them—earthly thinking people. It was people like this who

Conclusion

eventually beheaded John, and ultimately killed Jesus according to John 7:32: "The Pharisees heard the crowd whispering these things about Him, and the chief priests and the Pharisees sent officers to arrest Him."

Again "sent" to seize not to worship and serve, but sent eventually to arrest, as written in John 18:24: "So Annas sent Him bound to Caiaphas the high priest."

So, this is how the earthly would "send"—not as John, a man sent of God, not as Jesus, sent of the Father—but as men who beheaded John and bound Jesus.

Once again, He sends and says (Matthew 10:16), "Behold, I am *sending* you out as sheep in the midst of wolves; so be as wary as serpents, and as innocent as doves."

What are the systems of this world and the ways of this world? Who are the earthly people who would try to control our destiny, bind our minds and ways, and send their agents to hunt down, constrain, and destroy? The "wolves" of our society—those with human and worldly thinking. It is the wolves of circumstances and not faith. It is the Pharisees of religious rules and self-righteousness. It is people with limited reasoning. It is systems of democracy in churches, voting on the will and purposes of God, forgetting that when all is said and done, He is still the Supreme, the King of Kings, and the Ruler of this universe who directs, speaks with a prophetic voice across our land, and stands firm in His Word. He is the One and Only with all rights to the final word—He who commissions and by whom we indeed have been "Sent . . ."

As sheep being sent among wolves, should we be afraid? The answer is yes, as well as no. We need to have fear that would cause

SENT...

us to be as shrewd as serpents and innocent as doves, and yet, no because it is He who sends and He who promises:

> "All authority in heaven and on earth has been given to Me. Go, therefore, and make disciples of all the nations, baptizing them in the name of the Father and the Son and the Holy Spirit, teaching them to follow all that I commanded you; and behold, I am with you always, to the end of the age." —Matthew 28:18-20

Having covered this material, perhaps the "and behold, I am with you always" bears a new weight of revelation in what by and large encompasses a discharged commission, bathed in peace and confidence, that He Himself has proven and so prepared in us, as John 20:21 so inclusively states: "So Jesus said to them again, 'Peace be with you; as the Father has sent Me, I also send you.'"

> **"PEACE BE WITH YOU; AS THE FATHER HAS SENT ME, I ALSO SEND YOU."**

www.ingramcontent.com/pod-product-compliance
Lightning Source LLC
Chambersburg PA
CBHW050901160426
43194CB00011B/2241